P9-CRS-202

FOR CHILDREN'S PASTORS, CHRISTIAN EDUCATION DIRECTORS,
MISSIONS PROGRAM LEADERS AND TEACHERS OF KIDS IN GRADES 1-6

The Great KidMission

A COMPLETE RESOURCE TO EDUCATE AND EXCITE KIDS
ABOUT MISSIONS AROUND THE WORLD

MARY GROSS, EDITOR

Gospel Light

How to Make Clean Copies from this book

You may make copies of portions of this book with a clean conscience if:

◆ you (or someone in your organization) are the original purchaser;

◆ you are using the copies you make for a noncommercial purpose (such as teaching or promoting your ministry) within your church or organization;

◆ you follow the instructions provided in this book.

However, it is illegal for you to make copies if:

◆ you are using the material to promote, advertise or sell a product or service other than for ministry fund-raising;

◆ you are using the material in or on a product for sale;

◆ you or your organization are **not** the original purchaser of this book.

By following these guidelines you help us keep our products affordable.

Thank you,
Gospel Light

EDITORIAL STAFF

Editor, Mary Gross • **Associate Editor,** Linda Mattia • **Assistant Editor,** Kathleen McIntosh
Contributing Editors, David Arnold, Brad Bigney, Nancy Land
Designer, Carolyn Thomas • **Illustrators,** Steven Ordoñez, Chizuko Yasuda

Publisher, William T. Greig • **Senior Consulting Publisher,** Dr. Elmer L. Towns
Publisher, Research, Planning and Development, Billie Baptiste
Senior Editor, Lynnette Pennings, M.A.
Senior Consulting Editors, Dr. Gary S. Greig, Wesley Haystead, M.S.Ed.
Editor, Theological and Biblical Issues, Bayard Taylor, M.Div.

CONTENTS

Use these logos to help you choose appropriate activities:

YOUNGER ELEMENTARY

OLDER ELEMENTARY

ALL AGES

15 MINUTES

20 MINUTES

20-30 MINUTES

30-40 MINUTES

96837

GAMES 87

DRAMA 97

SNACKS 109

CLIP ART 117

APPENDIX 137

INDEXES 141

PREFACE

MISSIONS: Not what it used to be

Before the 1960's, understanding Christian missions was not terribly complex. Missions were generally perceived to be "overseas." Western "Christian" countries sent missionaries; non-western non-Christian countries received them (with varying degrees of hospitality or hostility). Generally, the fruits of missionary effort were non-western churches, perhaps too often considered fledglings not quite up to flying on their own—whether organizationally, financially, theologically or spiritually.

But today, western churches are seeing a vastly different missions reality! On the one hand, Christians are now truly a world family; no longer do "western" members predominate. The center of gravity in world Christianity has shifted from the north and west to the south and east. Two-thirds of the world's evangelicals are now in the "two-thirds world." Not only are there more non-western Christians in the world than westerners, but also, western missionaries are now outnumbered by missionaries from Asia, South America, Africa, and Oceania. The world's missions force of approximately 150,000 is half western and half "two-thirds world," now both to and from all seven continents.

In addition, Christian missions have been so successful in some countries that we are awed by the glorious power of God. One hundred years ago, everyone in Korea was Buddhist; in South Korea today, nearly 40 percent of the people profess faith in Christ. There, the five largest local churches in the world thrive. In Africa, it is estimated that 5,000 people each day turn to Christ. In Indonesia, tens of thousands have joined God's family, endangering their lives. In all its glorious diversity, the people of God are now joyfully declaring His glory in all the earth. No one culture now has a monopoly on missions, but every culture, renewed in Christ, has a significant gift to share with the worldwide body of Christ.

Does this mean that the church can rest easy now that Christianity is a genuine world religion? By no means! There are still approximately 11,000 people groups representing 2,500 major language groups that have no church. Further, there are often pockets of unreached ethnic groups in countries that otherwise might be considered "reached"— no longer does one necessarily go overseas to be a missionary.

The Great Commission includes establishing churches AND teaching believers "to obey everything I have commanded you" (see Matthew 28:18-20). It includes not only evangelistic efforts: Ministries of mercy and social justice are part and parcel of proclaiming the Gospel of the Kingdom. However, the basic goal of missions remains to establish indigenous, evangelizing, self-propagating and self-sustaining churches in every people group. How this might be accomplished, and what churches might look like in worship or practice in different cultures are open questions. Only after "missions" have established churches in given cultures can the larger "mission" of proclaiming the Kingdom of God be adequately addressed. Just because churches are established does not mean that the work is over.

MISSIONS: Communicating to Kids

How can we communicate a missions vision to kids? The first step is in preparing our own hearts. Every aspect of the program must then be committed to God in prayer—from which missionary to feature to each child who will attend. Then as we find out for ourselves what God is doing around the world, our understanding will increase and our ability to marvel at God's work will deepen. Excitement and gratitude for Christ's great salvation will shine in our eyes and show in our actions. Then we will be ready to teach—by example. Missions, like the other important things in life, are not taught so much as caught. Emil Brunner once noted that the Church exists by mission as burning exists by fire. If your heart is prepared, kids will see your excitement and sense your commitment. And you will communicate the most powerful and important aspects of missions to them.

USING THIS BOOK

Do any of these challenges crop up in your children's ministry?

"The Missions Conference is coming soon. How can we involve the children, too?"

"We'd love to see Vacation Bible School run longer— if we only had more material!"

"The Kids' Club members are asking questions about missions. We need to help them focus and learn while their interest is high."

The Great KidMission contains a huge variety of resources to help you create a customized five- to ten-day Children's Missions Conference, to extend Vacation Bible School or to enrich your Kids' Club and Sunday School programs.

Included are:
◆ Bible stories.
◆ Learning activities— crafts, drama and games.
◆ Forms for obtaining "live missions reports" from missionaries' kids around the world, other forms and ideas for missions resources.
◆ Clip art, reproducible patterns and maps.
◆ Snack recipes from around the world.

All of these resources are geared to help children become educated— and excited—about missions around the world.

Five missions themes are highlighted:
◆ prayer,
◆ evangelism,
◆ perseverance,
◆ helping and
◆ church growth.

And the lessons are completely flexible because you create each lesson by choosing activities from the smorgasbord of available options in each category. The person who knows your needs best—you!—can choose and assemble the parts of each day's program to fit your needs and time schedule.

However, if mix-and-match isn't your style, see pp. 25-26 for the Ready-Made Lesson Plan Options!

GETTING STARTED

Welcome to the wonderful world of *The Great KidMission*! In the following pages, you'll find the help you need to create a children's missions conference, to formulate an extension for Vacation Bible School, or to enrich your Sunday School or Kids' Club programs.

Take time now to look through the ideas in this section. For an effective program, you'll want to choose the activities you'll use well in advance. That way, you'll know exactly how many helpers you'll need, what forms need to be sent, what books need to be reviewed, what materials need to be gathered and what patterns need to be photocopied. Once you have a basic plan in hand, we hope you are inspired by this book to embellish upon it in creative ways that will best teach your kids about the heart and soul of missions!

Room for Missions

Imagine a large, empty room. Space for your program abounds! But an empty room says nothing. It's boring. So don't stop imagining! How can this empty room become a place that explodes with excitement—an inviting, invigorating place to learn about missions? The possibilities are as limitless as your imagination!

Of course, you'll need an area for story-telling, ample space for playing games, a craft area and perhaps a puppet stage or other feature. But Missions Center should be the first thing to catch the eye of anyone who enters the room (see p. 14). The Missions Center will be an area of the room in which kids can explore various aspects of missions, cultures or countries in a hands-on, kid-friendly way.

As you mentally map out the areas needed for your program and choose the countries or ministries you will feature, take time to consider the impact environment can have in bringing those countries or ministries to life! The look of the room itself can communicate enthusiasm about missions to your children!

Your learning space could be turned into:

♦ a computer-filled information station, with charts and maps hung on walls

♦ an outdoor marketplace, with festoons of fabric hung from the ceiling

♦ a teepee or a summer hogan, with butcher-paper outdoor murals on the walls

♦ a theater, with curtains made from old bed sheets and international costumes hung on a rack

♦ an old city, with a series of archways cut from refrigerator boxes and painted (or "stuccoed" with a sun-dried paste of Ivory soap flakes, food coloring and water).

Wear It!

There's nothing like a costume to gain attention! As you choose the countries to feature, keep in mind costume ideas. Local libraries should provide books that give simple costume ideas. A trip to a fabric store or thrift shop can provide inexpensive materials. Costumes may also be available from missionaries, foreign travelers or emigrants from the featured country. (To create an original African fabric, see p. 55.)

Consider recruiting an adult or teen as the "costume designer" who collects and assembles the needed clothing articles. If you can't find a costume in your size, recruit someone of the proper size to help by simply wearing the costume.

Bible-times costumes are also effective. Consider using them to help tell the Bible stories. Recruit several story tellers for the Bible stories (some stories are written in first person for easy telling). When the story teller dresses as the main character and tells the story in his or her own words, the Bible story comes to life!

Give children opportunities to create costumes for themselves—it will surely spark excitement! Here are some easy ways to help children create costumes:

Provide a general costume box. Start with lengths of fabric and old ties for belts. (Invite church members to donate these items.) For extra creative possibilities, add old costume jewelry and pieces of fake fur.

Several of the Crafts Around the World (pp. 53-78) produce ethnic jewelry or accessory items. Use these crafts to expand and personalize children's costumes.

KidMission Reports

You'll need the KidMission Report Form and sample cover letter on pp. 10-11.

Photocopy one report form for each missionary's child from whom you'd like to get information. Use the sample letter as a guide in writing to the missionary family to ask their help in returning information from their child or children.

To provide ample time for these forms to be completed and returned, send them well in advance of your KidMission program. Current reports from around the world bring a freshness and an immediacy to the program that nothing can equal!

These forms and letters can be mailed, but consider faxing them or sending them through electronic mail if you need them quickly. Even a long-distance phone call during which you write down the child's responses (with parents' permission) may be worth the expense if time is short.

Responses to the KidMission Report form may be used as a basis for some service projects or as an information source in the Missions Center. You may also choose to read KidMission Reports aloud as a feature item during Response Time or as the "hook" before a Bible story.

Books, Books, Books

As you prepare materials for your program, remember that great books can spark kids' interest in missions. Look for collections of short missionary biographies with vivid illustrations that could be made available at the Missions Center (see p. 16) for individual readings. Biography portions could also be read aloud during Response Time or as part of Bible Story Time.

Look, too, for resource books that focus children on praying for missions around the world. These can be an exciting asset; they grab kids' interest with pictures, country fact boxes, prayer needs of the country, maps and flags. Use them at the Missions Center (for use, see p. 15).

Check your church library for missionary biographies. Use the Book Talk Form (p. 12) to introduce the books available. If your schedule doesn't allow time for reading the Book Talks aloud, consider photocopying completed Book Talk Forms for kids to read individually. Set up a special "Visual Resource" table in the Missions Center for this. Or create audio Book Talks at the "Audio Resource" area of the Missions Center (see p. 15) for individual listening.

Your public library can provide many books (and video resources) about other countries, cultures and languages. Some public libraries also have biographies of missionaries. (Check the 200's—the religion section of the Dewey Decimal System—as well as the biography section.)

Donated back issues of *National Geographic* can provide another wonderful resource, both for information and for vivid photography.

FROM: Name: _____ Age: _____

Country: _____ City or region: _____

Language spoken here:

_____

How well do you speak the language? (Color in the boxes to tell.)

☐☐☐☐☐☐☐☐☐☐☐☐☐☐☐☐☐☐☐☐☐☐☐☐☐☐☐☐☐☐

(Not at all)   (Very well)

Do you have brothers or sisters?
Names:

Ages:

Do you have pets?

Tell us a way your country is different from ours:

What do you usually eat for breakfast?

What do you enjoy most about living in your country?

What do you like least about living in your country?

What's your favorite game? snack? book?

What kinds of jobs does your family do to tell the people in your country about the good news of Jesus? How do you help?

We'd like to pray for you. What can we pray about?

©1996 by Gospel Light. Permission to photocopy granted. **KIDMISSION REPORT FORM**

Date

Dear (Name of Missionary):

We are planning a special program at our church to teach children about missions. Our goal is to help children discover the importance of missions and to help them understand that we all can be involved in missions efforts by praying for and supporting missionaries.

With this in mind, we would like to have your child(ren) fill out the enclosed report form. We want to use this valuable information from your child(ren) as a way to help the children here pray for your child(ren) and write to them.

We would appreciate your returning the report forms to us by (date). After *The Great KidMission* program, we will send letters from the children here to your child(ren). If there are any particular needs or concerns not addressed on this report form that you would like us to pray about or help with, please feel free to add them on a separate sheet of paper.

Thank you for your time in helping your child(ren) with these reports and returning them to us. You are constantly in our thoughts and prayers.

In God's love,

(Leaders' names)
Kids' Mission Program Leaders
(Church's name, address)

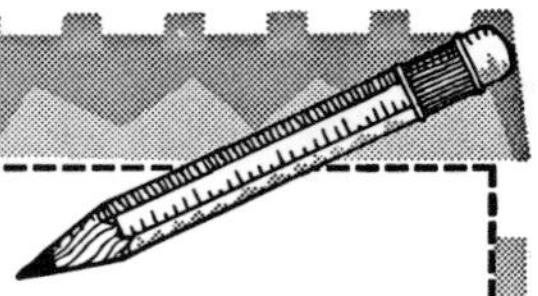

HOOK:

SAMPLE from the book:

SUMMARY:

SUBJECT:

AUTHOR:

PUBLISHER:

TITLE:

 BOOK TALK FORM

HOOK:
Amy Carmichael's first remembered prayer was for blue eyes. She had brown eyes and she desperately wanted blue ones like her mother's. She believed that God had heard her prayer but had answered no.

SAMPLE from the book:
Amy provided a home for children who were abused through cult temple practices in India. "The wisdom of Amy wearing Indian dress can clearly be seen as this young girl quickly identified with someone whose appearance looked comforting and reassuring. How much more the wisdom of God is evident in giving Amy the brown eyes she first despised! Amy appeared a natural "mother figure" to these distressed children, abandoned by their own parents....The years she had spent as the eldest of a large family helping her younger brothers and sisters, and the times she had trained youngsters in her Scripture Union classes at Broughton Grange bore rich fruit....the Lord was to grant her a profound emotional satisfaction in rescuing these children and bringing them up."

SUMMARY:
This young Irish woman made children feel safe and important. She worked in several very different places, as well as in her home town. During her missionary life she helped many children and still wrote 35 books!

SUBJECT:
Missionary to India whose life and writings continue to touch the world.

TITLE:
Amy Carmichael

AUTHOR:
Kathleen White

PUBLISHER:
Bethany House Publishers

THE MISSIONS CENTER

The Missions Center is the hands-on heart of your missions program. It's an area of the classroom that is staffed and ready for kids to use as they enter the room each day. In the Missions Center, kids have time to move freely from one feature area to the next. One child may use a computer to find information about a chosen country or listen to audio cassettes prepared with Book Talks in the Audio information Division. Another may make a map or taste a foreign food. The variety of activities you make available to kids will be defined by the Missions Center's physical space, available help and equipment—and your imagination! The goal is to create a place where each child can explore missions, cultures and countries in a variety of interactive, kid-friendly ways.

Creating the Center

To create an effective center, first plan which missionary, country or ministry you will present each day. Some (or all) features of the Missions Center should change daily, to keep interest high!

Plan for plenty of space: one end of a large meeting hall or classroom would be ideal. If space does not allow for a large Missions Center, consider placing it outside the room, perhaps in a courtyard or even in the church foyer.

Plan for at least four or five activities in the center each day. Some features, such as the Cartography Division (see below) might stay as a regular feature, so that everyone has the chance to make a map. Other features, such as a "Please Touch" Museum, might be available for only the session that features a particular culture.

Plan to maximize early arrival time by using the Missions Center. It can be a flexible-time activity. As children arrive, greet them and direct them to the center. There, the adults or teens are ready to guide children in prepared activities (see below). If the Missions Center is exciting and interesting, kids will be eager to visit it first every day!

Get Help!

After choosing the Missions Center themes for each day, recruit teens or adults to help:

◆ assemble the needed materials for the center each day (see ideas below)

◆ take charge of the daily setup and decorating

◆ at each part of the center while kids are present—to answer questions, help with activities, etc.

If one or more Missions Center helper wears clothing of the featured culture, so much the better!

Parts and Pieces

Here are some possible components for your Missions Center. Use these ideas to help you create a center customized for your group.

Consulate, Passport Division

You will need the Passport Pattern (p. 19), pencils or pens, date stamp, ink pad, other rubber stamps or adhesive seals, scissors, glue stick, instant-photograph camera and one teen or adult "consulate clerk."

Photocopy one Passport Pattern for each child. On a table near the entrance to the Missions Center, provide passports, pencils or pens, date stamp, ink pad, etc. to make every child's passport look "official."

A "consulate clerk" helps children fill out the passports, stamps the passports and takes an instant photo of each child. Clerk then cuts photo to fit the photograph space on the passport and glues it on. (Or child may draw a picture of him- or herself in the space.)

Finished passports are brought to the "consulate" every session to be stamped with a different stamp for each country featured or with a date stamp for every day of "travel" during the conference.

Computer Information Division

You will need a computer installed with encyclopedia software and an adult who can guide research, help with computer access and make sure everyone has a turn.

From a software encyclopedia, kids access information about a desired country and hear music or sounds from that country.

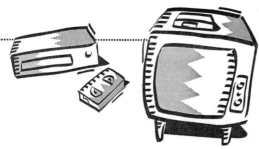

Kids may also use the computer to type E-mail messages to missionaries who have E-mail capabilities. (Save and download all messages to send later from an in-home computer linkup).

Video Information Division

You will need a television and VCR, travel videotapes about a featured culture (or videos about a particular ministry) and an adult or teen "video engineer."

Video clips could play continuously or at stated times—showing selected portions from travel videos or videos about a particular ministry or type of mission work.

With some prior notice, a featured missionary might be able to provide a short video about his or her work or send a video greeting to be played.

Audio Information Division

You will need prepared audiocassettes (see below), blank audiocassettes and cassette players.

Before the session, involve several children in preparing cassettes. Record (or assign an older child to record) children as they read information aloud from materials you have provided.

During Missions Center time, children may then listen to excerpts read aloud from a missionary's prayer letter, from encyclopedias or from magazine articles about the featured country.

In addition, children may also listen to music from the featured country or to a missions theme song for them to learn.

Audiocassette players may also be equipped with blank cassettes for children to use in creating an audio letter to send to a missionary. Children may sing, tell jokes or stories, recite a Bible verse, ask questions or tell about themselves on the cassette.

Research Division

You will need photocopies of the Fact Finder's Form (p. 17), the Completed Sample Fact Finder's Form (p. 18), books about a featured country (especially books with large, clear pictures), printed information from or about a missionary or ministry, paper and pencils. You may also wish to provide international airmail folders (aerogrammes).

Provide photocopies of the Fact Finder's Form, along

with the Completed Sample Fact Finder's Form. Children use provided books and information to answer the questions about the featured country.

If the Fact Finder's Form is above your group's ability, simply post several easy-to-answer questions about the featured country or missionary. (Ask both information-gathering questions and open-ended, "what do you think?" kinds of questions.) Challenge interested children to respond to the questions in writing. These responses could be read aloud anonymously as a feature during Response Time.

Interested children may also write down prayer requests after reading information from or about a missionary or ministry. Read these (anonymously) as part of your preparation for a time of prayer during Response Time.

Provide international airmail folders (aerogrammes). Interested children use them to write to the missionary whose information they have just read. Collect, address and mail these.

Food Division

You will need an adult or teen attendant, a table, small samples of the featured culture's food, napkins, a trash can and wet wipes (if hand-washing facilities are not nearby).

Before the session, find and prepare an appropriate ethnic food. Check the Ethnic Snacks section (p. 112) or encyclopedias and international cookbooks at local libraries.

This table could also feature a typical Third World meal (such as a small rice-and-bean or potato meal) as a way to introduce a ministry that deals with hunger relief.

Cartography Division

You will need Map of the World Patterns 1 and 2 (pp. 21-22), maps, atlases, pencils, felt pens, colored pencils and a "chief cartographer" (adult or teen volunteer).

Children use Map of the World Patterns and colored pencils or markers to highlight areas and locations of featured missionaries, places where a ministry has workers, etc.

Children may add geographical features (mountains, rivers, etc.) and names of continents, countries or cities. Children may make elaborate or simple maps, depending on their individual levels of ability and interest.

Please Touch Museum

You will need sturdy, touchable items from the countries or cultures you feature and an adult "museum docent" to guide conversation and spark imagination.

Children may look at, pick up and handle any item on the table. (If the docent is not familiar with the featured culture, provide an encyclopedia or other books from which he or she may help children find answers to their questions.)

Sample Table

If you are featuring a ministry to which children will donate items, you will need a sample collection of items needed for that project. Make up a sample box or bag for children to examine to help them understand what items are appropriate and needed for donation.

Other Possibilities

You will need several missionary biographies. Following the sample Book Talk Form (p. 12), create a written Book Talk for each book you wish to feature. Children can read the completed Book Talks to discover which of the books they would like to borrow for home reading. (Completed Book Talks can also be read during Response Time to interest children in reading missionary biographies.)

A Roving Missionary

You will need a missionary or members of a missionary family.

During Missions Center Time, the missionary (or family member) talks with children individually, answering questions about the country in which he or she lives and telling about his or her work.

Missionary Biography and Book Talk Table

Missions and Technology

The world is much smaller than it used to be! Missionaries leaving on a freighter for weeks of travel to the other side of the world, receiving no mail for months on end, are becoming a thing of the past. Of course, many missionaries still do travel to remote areas on foot, out of reach of most communications. But as technology has advanced, many missionaries are able to be reached in more ways—and more quickly—than by letter.

Electronic Mail:

Seek out the computer owners in your church who are connected to on-line services. If a missionary has a computer (or access to a computer) with the same E-mail capabilities, send and receive information through e-mail.

Fax Transmissions:

If your church has access to a fax line, send that telephone number to your missionary. Access to a fax machine may not be convenient on the missionary's end, but in times of emergency or urgent prayer need, the missionary may be able to find and use a fax machine to give your church an immediate message.

Shortwave Radio:

This is used a great deal worldwide but is sometimes overlooked in this country. Many "ham" (shortwave) radio operators have the capability to talk to other operators worldwide. And they are often enthusiastic about sharing their knowledge and telling their stories! Send messages to a missionary through a shortwave operator (or through several, to get from here to there!).

To find the ham in your church or the ham club in your area, look in the Yellow Pages under "shortwave radio equipment." Retailers will probably have information about local shortwave users.

International shortwave operators can also be a great speaking resource for your group. Even if the ham is not a Christian, his or her stories of international contact will spark excitement!

Some churches have even begun ham clubs of their own for the express purpose of ministering to and encouraging missionaries around the world!

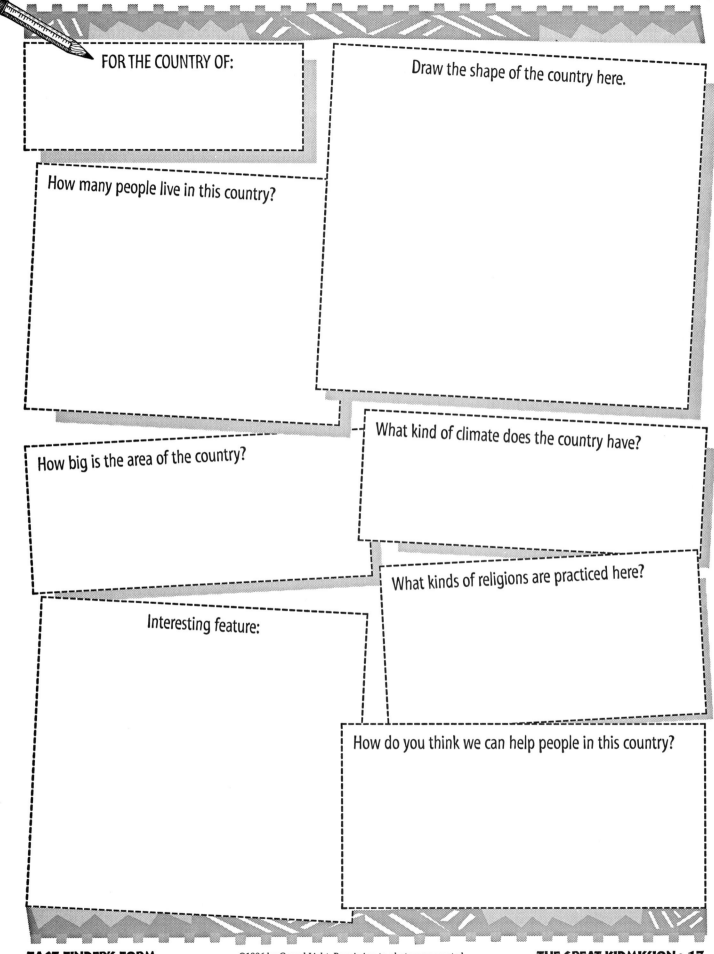

FOR THE COUNTRY OF:

Draw the shape of the country here.

How many people live in this country?

How big is the area of the country?

What kind of climate does the country have?

What kinds of religions are practiced here?

Interesting feature:

How do you think we can help people in this country?

FOR THE COUNTRY OF:

China

Draw the shape of the country here.

How many people live in this country?

21.3% of the world's population live in China—the country with the largest population in the world.

How big is the area of the country?

9,573,000 sq.km.—the third largest country in the world.

What kind of climate does the country have?

Varies. It's a very big country— sea coast, forests (cool); deserts (hot/cold)

Interesting feature:

Panda bears live here.

What kinds of religions are practiced here?

50% atheists, 30% Buddhist, Taoist or practice Confucianism, 6.1% Christian, and 13.9% Muslim, Animist, other.

How do you think we can help people in this country?

There is a movement to get Bibles to China, particularly children's illustrated Bibles. Pray for the Christians in China. Pray that the persecution of Christians will stop.

 FACT FINDER'S FORM (COMPLETED SAMPLE)

OFFICIAL PASSPORT
The Great KidMission

Name of Church: _____

Dates: _____

Building: _____

—FOLD—

NOTE: Cover these instructions and the words at the bottom of each page before you photocopy.

Make one two-sided photocopy from this pattern for each child (henceforth known as the Bearer).

Each Bearer receives a blank Passport from the Consulate, Passport Division, on the first day of travel. Bearer completes information and signs the passport.

Consulate date stamps the passport and adds official seals and stickers. At the beginning of each trip, Bearer presents passport for stamp or sticker to verify travel in that country.

The Great KidMission

This passport is valid only in the imaginations of *The Great KidMission* users.

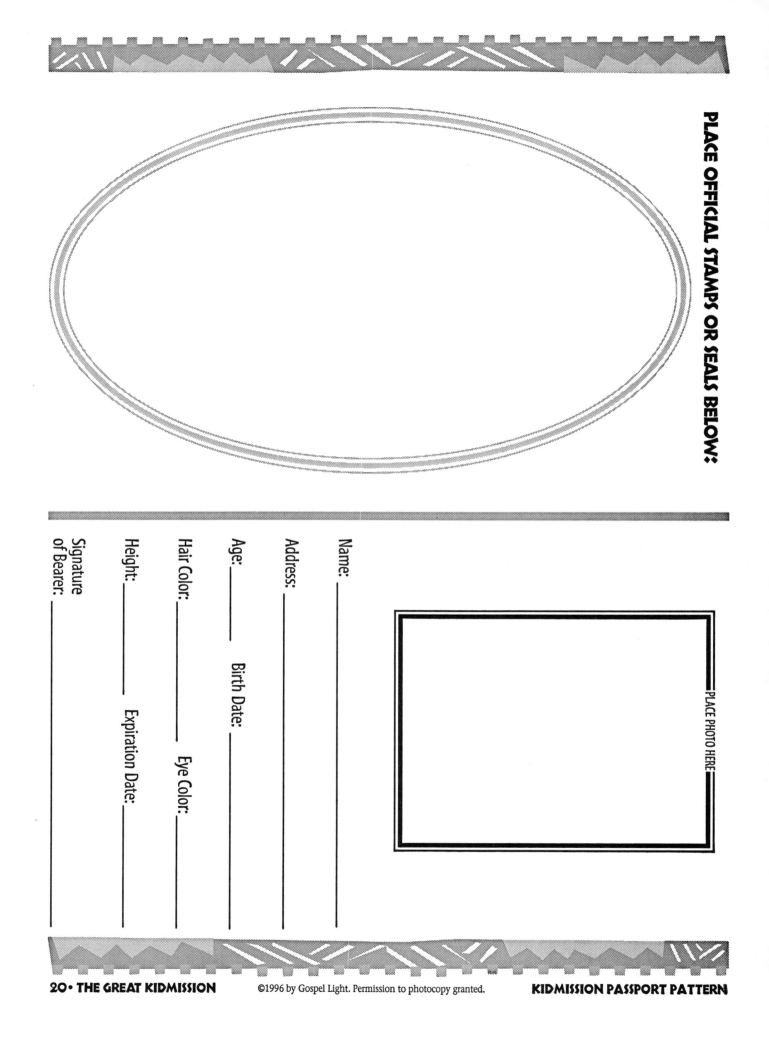

PLACE OFFICIAL STAMPS OR SEALS BELOW:

Name: _____

Address: _____

Age: _____ Birth Date: _____

Hair Color: _____ Eye Color: _____

Height: _____ Expiration Date: _____

Signature
of Bearer: _____

PLACE PHOTO HERE

KIDMISSION PASSPORT PATTERN

 MAP OF THE WORLD PATTERN 2

THE DAILY PROGRAM

Schedule

The schedule for every session should consist of at least the following parts:

◆ an activity to introduce children to the day's theme—preferably, time at the Missions Center. A Memory Moment game could also be used to introduce the memory verse. (Do both if time permits.)

◆ a Bible Story with appropriate discussion and application.

◆ a Missions Learning Activity time—activities that include games, crafts, snacks, service or drama projects.

◆ a Response Time, during which kids can worship and pray, reinforce the Bible story and share activities (skits, KidMission reports, Book Talks or Fact Finder's Forms from Mission Center activities).

Here's how a 60-minute schedule might look:

Missions Center Time	**10 minutes**
Memory Moment Game	**5 minutes**
Bible Story and Discussion	**15 minutes**
Drama, Craft or Game	**15 minutes**
Response Time	**15 minutes**

To accommodate a three-hour schedule:

Missions Center Time	**20 minutes**
Memory Moment Game	**15 minutes**
Bible Story and Discussion	**20 minutes**
Choice of Games or Drama Activities	**45 minutes**
Choice of Craft or Service Projects	**45 minutes**
Snack	**15 minutes**
Response Time	**20 minutes**

With some simple adaptations, the program can be customized to fit nearly every time frame.

This book is organized with indexes that make it easy to build a lesson from related activities for every session, so you can customize each session for maximum learning and fun!

KidMission Sessions can be organized in several ways:

♦ by highlighting the featured countries of missionaries your church supports;

♦ by emphasizing the five missions themes (see below);

♦ by focusing on individual missionaries or ministries.

Choices, Choices!

To focus a session on one country:

Choose a snack, a game and a craft from the featured country or another country in that area of the world. See Ready-Made Lesson Plan Options (p. 25).

Choose a Bible story and memory verse related to the theme (prayer, evangelism, perseverance, helping and church growth) that you wish to emphasize for that day.

Choose a Memory Moment Game (pp. 29-30) well-suited to your group (high or low degree of activity, high or low reading skill, etc.).

Focus the Missions Center on the chosen country; include information about missionary activity there.

To focus a session on one theme:

Choose a Bible story and memory verse related to the theme (prayer, evangelism, perseverance, helping or church growth) that you wish to emphasize for that day. Relate this story and its theme to situa- tions that specific mission- aries whom you know are currently experiencing.

Choose a Memory Moment Game (pp. 29-30) well-suited to your group (high or low degree of activity, high or low reading skill, etc.).

Choose a craft from the Missions Crafts (pp. 79-83) or from the Service Projects (pp. 84-86); relate these to the theme.

Choose a snack and game, perhaps related to a home country of the related ministries or missionaries.

Focus the Missions Center on ministries or mission- aries that relate to the chosen theme and the countries in which the missionaries work.

To focus on one missionary or ministry:

Choose a Bible story and memory verse related to prayer concerns or real-life situations that the featured missionaries or ministries are currently experiencing.

Choose a Memory Moment Game (pp. 29-30) well-suited to your group (high or low degree of activity, high or low reading skill, etc.).

For the craft, choose a service project that directly relates to the needs of the featured missionary or ministry.

Choose a snack and a game from the missionary or ministry's home country (or another country in that area of the world).

Focus the Missions Center on the featured missionary or ministry; include information about the home coun- try or countries of the missionary or ministry.

Notes on Mixing and Matching

Remember that children think in concrete, not ab- stract, ways. The younger the child, the more concrete the learning experience needs to be. They learn best when the ideas presented involve all of their senses—they need to see, hear, touch, taste and smell. With younger children, it's best to relate the ses- sions to countries or to specific missionaries. (Use of the KidMission Reports will help to make missionary life more real to children.) More abstract concepts such as the Bible-story theme or a focus on a large ministry is best left to upper-elementary children who can better grasp abstract ideas. As you mix and match activities, note the variety of age and skill levels indicated and use them in your planning. For instance, snacks vary in ease of preparation and some are better group activities than others. Game, craft and snack logos indicate the age groups for which they are most appropriate. With the help of an adequate number of adults, even the more challenging games or crafts can usually be enjoyed by all ages.

READY-MADE LESSON PLAN OPTIONS

Here are a series of preplanned programs for your perusal.
Use them as they are or look to them for inspiration in customizing your own program!

Ninety-Minute Program

Day One	Focus on Africa	Focus on Helping	Memory Verse
10 minutes	Memory Moment Game or Missions Center	Bag It (p. 29)	Deuteronomy 15:11
20 minutes	Bible Story	Lydia Shares (p. 44)	
20 minutes	Game	Egyptian Stick Race (p. 89)	
20 minutes	Snack	Banana in a Blanket (p. 110)	
20 minutes	Craft	African Rattle (p. 57)	

Day Two	Focus on Mexico	Focus on Evangelism	Memory Verse
10 minutes	Memory Moment Game or Missions Center	Calling You (p. 30)	John 3:16
20 minutes	Bible Story	New Feet and Good News (p. 34)	
20 minutes	Game	Tlachtli (p. 92)	
20 minutes	Snack	Burritos (p. 112)	
20 minutes	Craft	Mexican Piñata (p. 70)	

Day Three	Focus on Japan	Focus on Perseverance	Memory Verse
10 minutes	Memory Moment Game or Missions Center	Echo Me (p. 29)	Acts 22:15
20 minutes	Bible Story	Always a Missionary (p. 48)	
20 minutes	Game	Crab Race (p. 88)	
20 minutes	Snack	Japanese Pineapple Cream Dessert (p. 116)	
20 minutes	Craft	Japanese Origami (p. 69)	

Day Four	Focus on Russia	Focus on Church Growth	Memory Verse
10 minutes	Memory Moment Game or Missions Center	Keep the Beat (p. 30)	Matthew 28:19
20 minutes	Bible Story	Growing a Church (p. 50)	
20 minutes	Game	Gorelki (Russian Line Tag) (p. 90)	
20 minutes	Snack	Russian Two-Cheese Salad (p. 116)	
20 minutes	Craft	Russian Easter Eggs (p. 74)	

Day Five	Focus on Pacific Rim	Focus on Prayer	Memory Verse
10 minutes	Memory Moment Game or Missions Center	Line by Line (p. 30)	Romans 1:16
20 minutes	Bible Story	Answered Prayer at the Door! (p. 40)	
20 minutes	Game	Presohan (Filipino Tag) (p. 92)	
20 minutes	Snack	Chow Mein Chewies (p. 113)	
20 minutes	Craft	Vietnamese Lanterns (p. 78)	

THE GREAT KIDMISSION • 25

Three-Hour Program

Day One		Focus on Africa	Focus on Helping	Memory Verse
20 minutes	Missions Center		Africa	Deuteronomy 15:11
10 minutes	Memory Moment Game		Bag It (p. 29)	
20 minutes	Drama Activity		An International Incident (p. 101)	
20 minutes	Bible Story		Lydia Shares (p. 44)	
20 minutes	Service Project		Adopt a Missionary Kid (p. 84)	
20 minutes	Game		Egyptian Stick Race (p. 89)	
30 minutes	Snack		Banana in a Blanket (p. 110)	
20 minutes	Craft		African Rattle (p. 57)	
20 minutes	Response Time			

Day Two		Focus on Mexico	Focus on Evangelism	Memory Verse
20 minutes	Missions Center		Mexico	John 3:16
10 minutes	Memory Moment Game		Calling You (p. 30)	
20 minutes	Drama Activity		Gotta Tell! (p. 103)	
20 minutes	Bible Story		New Feet and Good News (p. 34)	
20 minutes	Service Project		Missionary Care Package (p. 85)	
20 minutes	Game		Tlachtli (p. 92)	
30 minutes	Snack		Burritos (p. 112)	
20 minutes	Craft		Mexican Piñata (p. 70)	
20 minutes	Response Time			

Day Three		Focus on Japan	Focus on Perseverance	Memory Verse
20 minutes	Missions Center		Japan	Acts 22:15
10 minutes	Memory Moment Game		Echo Me (p. 29)	
20 minutes	Drama Activity		Sound-Effects Story Drama (p. 99)	
20 minutes	Bible Story		Always a Missionary (p. 48)	
20 minutes	Service Project		Bread Dough Napkin Rings (p. 86)	
20 minutes	Game		Crab Race (p. 88)	
30 minutes	Snack		Japanese Pineapple Cream Dessert (p. 116)	
20 minutes	Craft		Japanese Origami (p. 69)	
20 minutes	Response Time			

Day Four		Focus on Russia	Focus on Church Growth	Memory Verse
20 minutes	Missions Center		Russia	Matthew 28:19
10 minutes	Memory Moment Game		Keep the Beat (p. 30)	
20 minutes	Drama Activity		I'm Gonna Be a Missionary (p. 106)	
20 minutes	Bible Story		Growing a Church (p. 50)	
20 minutes	Missions Craft		Invitation to Church (p. 82)	
20 minutes	Game		Gorelki (p. 90)	
30 minutes	Snack		Russian Two-Cheese Salad (p. 116)	
20 minutes	Craft		Russian Easter Eggs (p. 74)	
20 minutes	Response Time			

Day Five		Focus on Pacific Rim	Focus on Prayer	Memory Verse
20 minutes	Missions Center		Vietnam	Romans 1:16
10 minutes	Memory Moment Game		Line by Line (p. 30)	
20 minutes	Drama Activity		Guess Who's Coming to Dinner? (p. 104)	
20 minutes	Bible Story		Answered Prayer at the Door! (p. 40)	
20 minutes	Missions Craft		Missionary Prayer Calendar (p. 82)	
20 minutes	Game		Presohan (p. 92)	
30 minutes	Snack		Chow Mein Chewies (p. 113)	
20 minutes	Craft		Vietnamese Lanterns (p. 78)	
20 minutes	Response Time			

BIBLE MEMORY VERSES AND ACTIVITIES

The Word of God is living and powerful— the written story of the Living Word!

The Word of God gives us good news to tell every person, from our own neighbors to the most distant people groups. It's the indispensable guidebook of Christian missions around the world. There's nothing more important for kids to hide in their hearts!

This section begins with the theme Bible passage—The Great Commission. Since it is the basis for all missionary activity, it would be an effective reminder posted where it can be easily seen. Refer to it often to help kids connect Jesus' words with the emphasis on missions.

Also included are a selection of missions-related Bible verses, listed in order from simple to more complex. Choose to memorize either the theme Bible passage or a series of daily verses as a customized part of your program. (See Ready-Made Lesson Plan Options on p. 25 for some use suggestions.) Posting the memory passage or verse written out in large, clear letters will help children as they play the daily Memory Moment Games and help them better remember the verse.

THEME BIBLE PASSAGE

Matthew 28:18-20

Then Jesus came to them and said, "All authority in heaven and on earth has been given to me. Therefore go and make disciples of all nations, baptizing them in the name of the Father and of the Son and of the Holy Spirit, and teaching them to obey everything I have commanded you. And surely I am with you always, to the very end of the age."

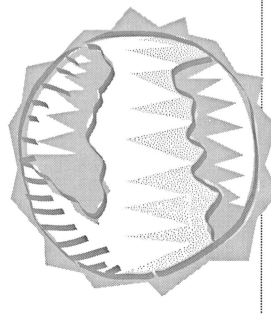

BIBLE MEMORY VERSES

These verses are listed in order from simple to complex to help you choose the most appropriate memory verses for your group.

Matthew 28:19
Go and make disciples of all nations.

Mark 16:15
Go into all the world and preach the good news to all creation.

Acts 22:15
You will be his witness to all men of what you have seen and heard.

Isaiah 43:10
"You are my witnesses," declares the Lord, "and my servant whom I have chosen."

Psalm 108:3
I will praise you, O Lord, among the nations; I will sing of you among the peoples.

Romans 1:16
I am not ashamed of the gospel, because it is the power of God for the salvation of everyone who believes.

Deuteronomy 15:11
I command you to be openhanded toward your brothers and toward the poor and needy.

1 John 4:14,15
The Father has sent his Son to be the Savior of the world. If anyone acknowledges that Jesus is the Son of God, God lives in him and he in God.

John 3:16
For God so loved the world that he gave his one and only Son, that whoever believes in him shall not perish but have eternal life.

Acts 1:8
But you will receive power when the Holy Spirit comes on you; and you will be my witnesses in Jerusalem, and in all Judea and Samaria, and to the ends of the earth.

MEMORY MOMENT GAMES

Here are 11 fairly short games that can help your group plant the Bible Memory Verses in their hearts. Try using one Memory Moment Game during each session to draw children's interest and help them remember the session's Scripture. Remember, children aren't passive observers. They learn best by doing!

Bag It

YOUNGER ELEMENTARY

Materials: Bibles, sheets of paper, felt pen, beanbag.

Preparation: Letter the words to the Bible Memory Verse on sheets of paper, one word or short phrase for each sheet. Lay sheets in mixed-up verse order on the floor.

Play: Children take turns tossing the beanbag onto papers. When beanbag lands on a paper, child picks up the paper on which the beanbag landed. When all papers are picked up, help children put words or phrases in verse order, using their Bibles as a reference. Repeat game as time permits.

Echo Me

ALL AGES

Materials: Chalkboard and chalk or large paper and felt pen.

Preparation: Letter the words to the Bible Memory Verse on a chalkboard or large sheet of paper. Place it where it is easily seen.

Play: Say the first word of the verse; children echo. Say the next two words, then the next three words, etc. Children echo each group of words, then repeat entire verse together. Invite children to repeat verse in similar fashion, giving you time to echo their word groupings. Invite several children to be leaders as time permits.

Pass the Word

ALL AGES

Materials: Index cards, felt pen, cassette player with music cassette or CD player and audio disc. Optional—spring-type clothespins.

Preparation: Letter each word of the Bible Memory Verse on a separate index card; if verse is long, letter several words on one card. Number the cards in verse order.

Play: Give each card to a child. As music plays, children pass cards around the circle. When music stops, children holding cards read them in verse order, using the numbers on the cards. After playing several rounds, children holding cards come to the front and arrange themselves in verse order. Repeat the verse together several times.

Challenge: Each child uses a spring-type clothespin to pass the cards around the circle.

Make a Motion

ALL AGES

Materials: Chalkboard and chalk or large paper and felt pen.

Preparation: Letter the words to the Bible Memory Verse on a chalkboard or large sheet of paper. Place it where it is easily seen.

Play: Sit in a circle. Begin the game by making a hand motion as you say the first word of the Bible Memory Verse aloud. Child seated next to you repeats your motion and word, then adds a different motion as he or she says the second word of the verse. Continue until all words of the verse have been used. Then repeat verse all together several times, using the hand motions. (Note: Motions need not represent the meanings of the words.)

Mirror Writing

YOUNGER ELEMENTARY

Materials: Index cards, mirrors, paper, pencils, felt pen.

Preparation: Letter each word of the Bible Memory Verse backward on a separate index card with felt pen. (You may wish to also letter the words to the verse on large paper for children's reference.)

Play: Provide several mirrors and invite children to take turns reading the words in the mirror. Each child may copy down the "decoded" words, then put them in verse order.

Join Me

YOUNGER ELEMENTARY

Materials: Index cards, felt pen.

Preparation: Letter each word of the Bible Memory Verse on a separate index card. (You may wish to letter the words to the verse on a large sheet of paper for children's reference.)

Play: Sit on the floor facing group. Place all cards on the floor behind you. Hold a card in each hand; put your hands behind your back. Invite children to choose one of the cards in your hand by saying "left" or "right." As child takes card, he or she holds it up for the group to read. After all cards are distributed, children hold up their cards and place themselves in verse order. Repeat verse together several times. Repeat game as time permits.

Calling You

ALL AGES

Materials: Bible, blindfold, chalkboard and chalk or large paper and felt pen.

Preparation: Letter the words to the Bible Memory Verse on a chalkboard or large sheet of paper. Place it where it is easily seen.

Play: Repeat the verse several times together, then ask for a volunteer to be blindfolded. The blindfolded child counts to 10 while the others tiptoe around an open area. Blindfolded child calls out the first half of the Bible Memory Verse (for example, "Go into all the world" if the verse is Mark 16:15). Other children freeze in place and answer with the second half of the verse ("and preach the good news to all creation."). Children stay frozen and continue to respond with the second half of the verse whenever blindfolded child calls with the first half of the verse. As blindfolded child hears the responses, he or she moves around to locate and tag a child who is frozen. Frozen child becomes the caller and game continues as time permits.

Keep the Beat

ALL AGES

Materials: Chalkboard and chalk or large paper and felt pen.

Preparation: Letter the words to the Bible Memory Verse on a chalkboard or large sheet of paper. Place it where it is easily seen.

Play: Say the verse aloud together several times, concentrating on the rhythm of the words. Then invite children to think of rhythmic actions to do along with the verse (such as claps, finger snaps, patting knees, stamping feet, etc.). Mark *X* for claps, *S* for snaps, etc. beneath verse words on large paper. Invite children to do the rhythmic actions as you say the verse slowly aloud. Then repeat the verse aloud several times together, adding first just the claps, then the snaps, and so on until all the rhythmic actions shown are being used. Continue as time permits.

Line by Line

ALL AGES

Materials: Chalkboard and chalk or large paper and felt pen.

Preparation: Letter the words to the Bible Memory Verse on a chalkboard or large sheet of paper, dividing the verse into phrases of a few words each. Starting with the first phrase, letter *1* for the first group beside the first phrase, *2* for the second group beside the second phrase and so on, alternating the two groups' parts. Place verse where it is easily seen.

Play: Children repeat verse together once or twice, then count off as *1* or *2*. Gather each group on opposite sides of the room to say the verse in a call-and-response fashion. Count children off again and separate the new groups to repeat the verse again. After two rounds, invite two volunteers (one from each group) to say the verse phrases as written, then to say the whole verse together without looking.

Picture This

ALL AGES

Materials: Bibles, chalkboard and chalk or large paper and felt pen.

Preparation: Letter the words to the Bible Memory Verse on a chalkboard or large sheet of paper, leaving large blank spaces for words that children can illustrate. Place the sheet where it is easily seen.

Play: Children find the Bible Memory Verse in their Bibles and tell which words are missing from the verse on the paper. In the blank spaces, children draw pictures to represent the missing words. (Missing words may be illustrated in more than one way.) If your group is large, divide group into teams of four to six children and prepare a rebus paper for each team. Invite children to tell about their illustrations, if they wish. When all pictures have been drawn, repeat the verse together several times.

Enrichment Idea: Children create gestures to illustrate missing words. "Gesture illustrators" stand in front to help others remember the gestures as you repeat the verse several more times.

Verse Volley

ALL AGES

Materials: Chalkboard and chalk or large paper and felt pen, balloons of varying sizes and shapes—one for every two children.

Preparation: Letter the words to the Bible Memory Verse on a chalkboard or large sheet of paper. Place it where it is easily seen.

Play: Group children into pairs and give each pair a balloon. Pairs blow up balloons and tie them closed. (Help as needed.) As children in each pair bat the balloon back and forth, they repeat the words of the verse, one word for each bat. If a balloon hits the ground, the pair begins the verse again. Challenge children to see if they can repeat the entire verse without stopping, then to repeat it three or more times without stopping. After each round, invite children to trade balloons so everyone gets a turn with balloons of different sizes and shapes.

Enrichment Idea: Children use only certain body parts to bat balloon: elbows and knees, heads and shoulders, etc. If space is limited, partners kneel or sit cross-legged to bat balloon.

BIBLE STORIES

Everyone loves to hear a good story! And good missions stories help us see God's love in action. The book of Acts is not only a missions handbook, but also a source for some of the most exciting missions stories ever! These stories tell some of the highlights of early missionary work found in the book of Acts.

The following Bible stories focus on five missions themes of prayer, evangelism, perseverance, church growth and helping. Two of the stories are told from a first-person viewpoint. For variety, consider inviting a story teller, dressed in Bible-times costume, to tell these stories. Presenting Bible stories in a variety of ways keeps attention high!

POWER TO TELL THE WORLD

The very first church begins to grow.
Matthew 28:16-20; Acts 1:1-14; 2:1-42

Tell me about the hardest job anyone has ever given you to do. (Volunteers tell.) **Listen to find out what exciting job Jesus gave to His friends!**

After Jesus died and rose again, He met with His followers many times. When Jesus met with His friends, He told them that He would soon return to heaven. He also told them to wait in Jerusalem, because He was going to send the Holy Spirit to help them.

Forty days after His resurrection, Jesus led a group of followers to the Mount of Olives. Some of them asked Him if He'd soon become their king. Jesus replied that they weren't supposed to know that.

He went on to tell them that after He left they would have power to tell others about Him in Jerusalem, Judea, Samaria—and all over the whole world.

He told them, "All power has been given to Me. So go and make disciples of all people, baptizing them and teaching them to obey what I have taught you. And I will be with you always."

As soon as He finished speaking, Jesus rose up through the clouds and out of sight! His friends were amazed! They stood and stared up into the sky. As they gazed upward, two angels appeared.

"Why are you standing here staring up into the sky?" the angels asked. "Jesus has left earth and gone back to heaven. And some day He will come back—in the same way He went to heaven."

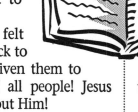

Jesus' followers must have felt stunned as they made their way back to Jerusalem. What a job Jesus had given them to do—to go and make disciples of all people! Jesus wanted them to tell EVERYONE about Him!

There are so many people just in Jerusalem, not even counting Judea and Samaria, the disciples might have thought. *And tell the rest of the world about Jesus? How will we EVER get the job done?*

But Jesus had promised that He would send the Holy Spirit to help them. So the believers prayed and waited for Jesus to keep His promise.

The Holy Spirit Comes

It was now almost a month and a half—50 days—since the time when Jesus was crucified. It was time for another Jewish holiday, Pentecost. Jerusalem was jammed with people who had come to celebrate Pentecost. Jesus' followers were gathered in a room, praying together. Suddenly, a sound like blowing wind filled the room where they were. What looked like small flames hovered above the head of each person. Now the Holy Spirit had come!

A Crowd Gathers

Along with the sound of wind and the flames, the Holy Spirit gave all the people in the room an amazing ability. They could speak in languages they had never learned! Soon they were spilling out into the street, talking excitedly in a dozen languages! It was a miracle! A crowd gathered, curious to see what was going on.

There were people from all over the world in that crowd. As they listened, they looked at each other in amazement—for each person in the crowd was hearing about Jesus in the language of the country in which he or she was born!

"How can this be?" they asked each other. "These people are from Galilee. How can they speak the languages of our homelands?"

Others said, "These people are drunk! They're talking nonsense."

But Peter stood up to speak. The Holy Spirit had given Peter and the other believers power and boldness, as Jesus had promised. Peter said, "Listen, all of you, we're not drunk. It's only nine o'clock in the morning. No, what is happening right here before you was predicted hundreds of years ago by the prophet Joel. Joel said that God would pour out His Spirit on all people." (See Joel 2:28,29.)

Peter continued, "Jesus of Nazareth came and lived among you. He did miracles and showed many signs and wonders. He was the Messiah. You all knew Him and you have wickedly killed Him." Peter also told about King David's prophecies of Jesus' coming.

"And so," Peter continued, "if David were here today, he would say that Jesus is truly the Messiah. And now I'm telling you that God raised Jesus from the dead and for forty days we have seen Him and talked with Him. And He has given us the Holy Spirit. His Spirit is now helping us to speak in different languages."

The New Church

In the crowd, there were people who had hated Jesus, people who had cried, "Crucify Him! Crucify Him!"

These people could have become angry at what Peter had said. But they didn't!

God's Spirit used Peter's message to open the people's minds and hearts. They were ashamed for what they had done. They cried out, "What should we do?" Peter said, "Repent, and be baptized in the name of Jesus and be forgiven for your sins."

Guess what happened? THREE THOUSAND people said, "Yes, we believe! God, forgive us for what we have done to your Son!" And that day THREE THOUSAND people became members of God's family!

These new believers listened to God's Word and to the teaching of the disciples. They gathered in the Temple, ate together, prayed together and praised God together. Every day more people were added to the church. Jesus had sent the Holy Spirit as He had promised. With His help, they really COULD do the job Jesus had given them to do!

Use the questions below after telling the Bible story, during activity times or as part of Response Time.

1.
What promises did Jesus make?
(I will be with you. I will send the Holy Spirit. You will have power to witness.)

2.
In what ways did the believers know the Holy Spirit had come?
(Sound of wind. Flames. Ability to speak other languages. Boldness.
Unbelievers understood the truth about Jesus and wanted to be forgiven and know Jesus.)

3.
What are some ways God's Spirit helps the church to grow today?
Are they the same or different from when the Holy Spirit first came?
(People learn the truth about Jesus and want to be forgiven and know Him.
The Holy Spirit helps people to tell others about Jesus.)

4.
What are some ways God's Spirit helps you today?
(Helps me tell others about Jesus. Gives me love for others because Jesus loves them.)

NEW FEET AND GOOD NEWS

**A man who was once lame tells how God's power
helped him and the people who saw his new feet!**

Acts 3:1-26

By the shadows, I could tell that it was afternoon. There were fewer people coming by now, passing me on their way through the Temple gate. But since it was Temple law that Jewish people should give some money to beggars like me, I waited patiently. I shook my cup and tried to get the people to look at me.

How many years had I been carried to this same spot to beg? So much time had passed that I couldn't remember. Thousands of people had walked past me through this gate. Everyone else had feet and legs that worked. They could go places and earn money for food and things they needed. But me—what could I do? I couldn't even stand up. I would have given anything to be able to walk!

Two Who See Me

A few more people walked by. There still wasn't much money in my cup so I called out, "Money, money for a poor crippled man!"

Clink, clink went two small coins into my cup. People didn't even look at me or speak to me. They had gotten tired of seeing me here day after day—helpless and asking for money. There wasn't even enough money in my cup to buy food. It hadn't been a very good day. But two men were heading toward me. They were looking at me—right into my eyes! *Surely they will give me some money!* I thought. They kept on looking at me. *Who can they be?* I wondered.

"Look at us!" one said to me.

I WAS looking at them. They looked kind. *They will give me money,* I thought.

"I don't have any money to give you," the man continued. "But what I do have I will give to you. In the name of Jesus of Nazareth, stand up and walk!" I looked at him in amazement as he took my hand and pulled me to my feet. And then my own feet and legs—that had never worked—suddenly felt STRONG! My toes moved! My knees bent! I WALKED! I was so happy that I began jumping and running. It felt wonderful to leap into the air and feel the wind in my hair.

"PRAISE GOD!" I shouted over and over. Then I ran to the two men. Their names were Peter and John. I walked along with them as they went to the Temple. I couldn't believe what had happened to me! I, the crippled beggar, was walking along with these men on feet that seemed brand-new! They worked perfectly—as if nothing had ever been wrong with me!

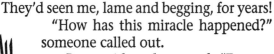

Peter Tells the Good News

People I had seen day after day, people who had known me all my life, stared as I walked into the Temple with Peter and John. Some looked shocked and angry. Others were amazed. Some blinked their eyes and looked at me again. I wanted everyone to know that Peter and John had helped me. And I kept praising God for healing me! Soon everyone crowded around Peter and John and me. They wanted to know what was going on! How was it that I was walking? They'd seen me, lame and begging, for years!

"How has this miracle happened?" someone called out.

Peter said to the crowd, "Do you think we made this man's legs and feet well by our own power? We are only men, just like you. It is Jesus—the Son of the God of Abraham, Isaac and Jacob—who has healed this man!"

Peter went on to tell the people all about Jesus. He told them how Jesus had died for all the wrong things that people do. He told them how Jesus is alive again. The people listened to every word Peter said because they could see that my new feet were a miracle! The people and I all learned about how much Jesus loves us and how we can know Him.

God helped Peter and John to tell the people about Jesus. They were some of the first missionaries! But Peter and John did more than just talk about God's power. They showed God's love and power when they stopped and helped me. And because God HEALED

me, everyone was curious to hear what they had to say. So they got to tell MORE people the good news of Jesus! Now, not only could I walk and run, but all of us heard the BEST news: that Jesus makes it possible for our sins to be forgiven. And we can ALL be a part of God's family!

Use the questions below after telling the Bible story, during activity times or as part of Response Time.

1.
What was wrong with the man by the gate?
(He couldn't walk.)

2.
What did Peter do when he saw the beggar?
(Stopped and helped him.)
Who healed him?
(Jesus.)
What did the people in the crowd do?
(They listened to Peter and John.)
Why?
(Because they had seen this miracle.
They were curious to hear what Peter and John had to say.)

3.
What are some ways missionaries tell people about Jesus today?
(Some perform songs or plays to get people's attention.
Some talk on TV or radio to tell about Jesus.
Some pray for people or help them as Peter and John did.)

FROM PERSECUTOR TO MISSIONARY

How God's power made an enemy into a friend.
Acts 9:1-22

After Jesus rose from the dead and went to heaven, there were many, many people in Jerusalem who became His followers. But soon following Jesus became very difficult! Jerusalem became especially dangerous for Christians—because of a man named Saul.

Saul lived in Jerusalem. He had been taught since he was a boy to obey all of God's laws. He was even a member of a strict religious group, the Pharisees. The Pharisees worked very hard to obey all of God's laws. As Saul studied about God and His laws, Saul learned that God had promised to send a Messiah—One who would make it possible for everyone's sins to be forgiven. Saul must have hoped that God would send the Messiah soon.

One day, Saul heard people saying that God had already kept His promise. They said that Jesus was the promised Messiah. But Saul didn't believe it! He didn't think Jesus really was the Savior. And if Jesus WASN'T the promised Messiah, then Jesus' followers were wrong. They would have to be stopped!

Saul Causes Trouble

One day, some people in Jerusalem became so upset at Jesus' followers that they grabbed one of them named Stephen. They dragged Stephen out of the city and killed him. Saul watched them do it. And he did nothing to stop them. In fact, he approved of what they did. Soon, he began doing everything he could to stop Jesus' followers.

Saul didn't waste any time. He gathered some other men and they marched from house to house. Any follower of Jesus they could find was dragged off to jail! Because Saul thought he was doing right, he didn't care if the people were frightened or even hurt!

Now Jerusalem wasn't the only place where people were becoming followers of Jesus! Many of Jesus' followers had moved away from Jerusalem to other cities.

Damascus was one of the big cities to which some of Jesus' followers had moved. It didn't take long for the good news of Jesus to begin spreading in Damascus. Instead of being destroyed, the church grew and grew and GREW!

Saul was furious when he heard about this new church in Damascus. He knew that merchants and traders from all over the world traveled through Damascus. *If these beliefs about Jesus grow in Damascus,* Saul may have thought, *there will be no stopping it.*

On to Damascus

Saul decided to arrest the believers who lived in Damascus, take them back to Jerusalem and throw them into jail. Soon Saul and his helpers were on their way. They traveled for almost a week to reach Damascus.

But just before they reached the city, the sky suddenly blazed with a light brighter than the sun! Saul fell to the ground in a panic. He couldn't see! What was happening?

Just then Saul heard a voice. "Saul," the voice said, "why are you persecuting Me, doing things against Me?"

"Who are you, Lord?" Saul asked, trembling. "I am Jesus, the One you are trying to hurt," the voice answered. "Get up and go into the city. Wait there. Someone will tell you what to do."

Then the light vanished. The voice spoke no more. The road to Damascus once again looked like it did on any other day. But EVERYTHING had changed for Saul!

Saul managed to stand up and open his eyes, but all he saw was darkness. He was BLIND! Saul's helpers gathered around him and helped him to the house where they were to stay. For three whole days Saul refused to eat or drink and was still blind.

Ananias Visits Saul

Meanwhile, in another house in Damascus, God spoke in a vision, or special dream, to a follower of Jesus who was named Ananias.

"Ananias," the Lord said, "go to Saul. He is praying. I want you to pray for him and he will be able to see again."

Ananias was amazed! "Lord," he exclaimed, "Saul is the enemy of all who believe in you. I've heard he's come here to arrest people who follow Jesus!"

"Go! Everything will be all right!" the Lord answered. "I've chosen Saul for an important job—telling the good news about Me to many people."

Even though Ananias must have felt frightened, he obeyed the Lord and went to the house where Saul was staying.

"Saul," Ananias said, "Jesus, who appeared to you on the road, has sent me here so that you can see again and be filled with the Holy Spirit." As Ananias placed his hands on Saul, something like fish scales fell from Saul's eyes. Suddenly, he could see! And Ananias could see something, too. He could see that Saul had changed from an enemy to a friend. To show he was now a believer in Jesus, the Messiah, Saul was baptized.

A New Missionary

The news about Saul spread like wildfire throughout Damascus! Instead of arresting Christians, Saul now spent his time preaching that Jesus is God's Son.

He had become a missionary! Jesus' followers must have praised God! Everyone who heard Saul preach was amazed at what he had to say. The man who had persecuted Jesus' followers, who had tried his hardest to stop God's family, was now telling everyone the good news that Jesus is God's Son!

NOTE: Not long after this, Saul took on a new name. He began to use the name Paul, which is a Roman name. And Paul is the name by which this missionary became famous!

Use the questions below after telling the Bible story, during activity times or as part of Response Time.

1.
What do you think Jesus' followers did when they heard Saul was coming?
(They may have prayed. They may have hidden to escape persecution.)

2.
Tell what happened to change Saul.
(Jesus told Saul to stop persecuting Him and His followers. Saul was blinded.)

3.
Who prayed for Saul?
(Ananias.)
What important job can you do to help missionaries?
(Pray. Make a prayer reminder. Write your prayers in a journal and see how God answers.)

GOOD NEWS FOR EVERYONE!

Peter learns that the good news of Jesus is for all people.
Acts 10—11:18

After Jesus went back to heaven, His friends began to tell other people about Him.

Now, most of these new missionaries were Jewish people. Many, many years before, God had chosen the Jews as His own special people. And they were not used to talking to people who were not Jews. They had even made laws about not talking to or being with Gentiles—any people who aren't Jews. So it seemed to them that they should tell only other Jewish people about the Messiah, Jesus.

So, even though Jesus had told His followers to teach ALL people about Him, only Jewish people were hearing the good news at first. But God wanted to send the good news to Gentiles, too! So God chose Peter to help the new missionaries understand. But even Peter had to be convinced.

Missionary Available

Peter was in a town called Joppa, teaching new believers about Jesus. Meanwhile, in another city some miles away, there lived a man named Cornelius. He was a Gentile, a commander in the Roman army. And he loved God and wanted to know more about God. One day while Cornelius was praying, an angel appeared!

"Cornelius," said the angel.

Cornelius stared. He stammered, "What is it, Lord?"

The angel answered, "Send some men to Joppa to bring back a man named Simon who is called Peter. He is staying with Simon the Tanner."

Cornelius quickly called two of his servants and a trusted soldier. He sent them off to find Peter.

Peter's Dream

While these three Gentile men traveled to bring Peter to Cornelius, God had to get Peter ready for them! Remember, Jewish law said Peter should not welcome these Gentile men, let alone travel with them to see another Gentile! Here's how God got Peter ready:

At about noon the next day, the three Gentiles were nearing Joppa. Peter was up on the roof of Simon's house.

I'll wait here until lunch is ready, he thought. He began to pray. While he was praying, he saw something that looked like a large sheet coming down from heaven. In the sheet were all kinds of animals and reptiles and birds—even animals and birds that Jewish people never, ever ate!

Then Peter heard a voice. "Get up, Peter," the voice said. "Kill and eat."

Peter was horrified! Jewish law said these animals were "unclean." A Jewish person was NEVER to eat their meat!

"Oh, no, Lord!" Peter cried. "I have never in my entire life eaten anything unclean!"

"Don't call anything unclean that God has made clean!" the voice said.

Three times Peter saw the same thing. Then it was over. The sheet with the animals was gone. While Peter sat there trying to understand what this meant, two things happened almost at once. The voice spoke to Peter again saying, "Simon, three men are looking for you. Get up and go with them, for I have sent them."

Downstairs, the men Cornelius had sent knocked at the gate!

"Is there a man named Peter here?" they asked.

In a flash, Peter understood! His dream about the animals meant that God did not think the Gentile people were unclean—in fact, God loved them! And if God loved Gentiles, Peter should, too!

Peter hurried down the stairs. "I'm the man you are looking for," he said. "What brings you here?"

"Cornelius, a Roman army officer in Caesarea, has sent us," the men replied. "He loves and fears God. Yesterday, an angel told him to bring you to his house to tell him about God."

Peter invited the men into the house—even though they were Gentiles. He gave them food and invited them to spend the night—even though yesterday, he would NEVER have done this!

The next morning Peter and the three Romans

started traveling back to Caesarea. Some believers from Joppa went along, too.

Peter Preaches to Gentiles

When Peter and the group arrived, Cornelius and his family AND his friends were all gathered, waiting, for Peter! Peter looked around at all the people gathered at Cornelius's house and said, "You know it is against Jewish law for a Jew to visit a Gentile. But God has shown me that I shouldn't call anyone unclean. That's why I came here. Now, why did you send for me?" Peter asked.

Cornelius told Peter about the angel. "We are ready to listen to everything God wants you to tell us," Cornelius said.

"Now I understand," Peter said. "God loves and accepts people from EVERY nation!"

So Peter began to tell all the Gentiles gathered there about Jesus. He told them how God sent His son, Jesus, to teach people about God and that even though Jesus was sent to earth by God, and even though He did only good everywhere He went, He was crucified. But after three days God raised Jesus from the dead. "Many of us saw Him after His resurrection—we talked and even ate with Him. He commanded us to tell the good news that EVERYONE who believes in Him is forgiven of sin," Peter said.

That's as far as Peter got. For just then, the Holy Spirit came to everyone who was listening! They began speaking in different languages and praising God—in just the same way as the Jews had on the day of Pentecost!

Peter and the Jewish believers stood there amazed. There was no doubt about it. The Holy Spirit had come to the Gentiles, too! God loved them just like He loved the Jews! After great rejoicing, Peter baptized all the new believers. They stayed for a few days, teaching them and worshiping God together. Now it was clear—God wanted the missionaries to bring the good news of Jesus to everyone—Jews and Gentiles, too!

Use the questions below after telling the Bible story, during activity times or as part of Response Time.

1.
Why did Peter need to know it was OK to be with Gentiles?
(Because he had grown up learning that Jewish people
and Gentile people were not to do things together.)

2.
Which people might be hard for you to love?
(People who don't like you. People who do things differently than you do.
People whom your friends don't like.)

3.
What are some ways you can show God's love to them?
(Be friendly. Include them in what you do. Help them, if a time comes when help is needed.
Share the good news about Jesus with them.)

ANSWERED PRAYER AT THE DOOR!

How Rhoda learned that God answers prayer.
Acts 12:1-18

Frightening Times

Today seemed like it was going to be one of the worst days of my life! First of all, we're celebrating the Passover. So for me, Rhoda, there's lots of extra work—because it's a feast day. And I'm a servant girl. I don't mind that, really. But the other reason this started out to be a terrible day is because we got some FRIGHTENING news: Herod, the Roman ruler, just had a Christian KILLED! You see, I'm a Christian, too! So you can imagine how nervous I was feeling. All the Christians were wondering what Herod would do next!

Mary (she's the lady I work for) had invited Peter to come and share the feast dinner with us. Peter's famous. He's a missionary! And he is a friend of Jesus. Peter travels around telling many people about Jesus. We were all glad to see him! But right while I was serving dinner, Roman soldiers BURST into the house! They arrested Peter and took him away. It was horrible. We were all afraid that Peter would be killed, too.

Mary had also invited many other Christians to her house. So as soon as Peter was gone, guess what we did? That's right! We prayed! We prayed with all our might to God, begging Him to protect Peter. It was hard to pray about anything except Peter!

A Knock at the Door

We prayed and prayed. Sometime later that same night, all of us were still together, praying for Peter. I heard a knock on the door. Uh-oh! Guess whose job it is to answer the door? That's right! So up I went to the heavy wooden door. I was nervous about who might be on the other side of the door. So I didn't open the door. Instead I called out, "Who's there?"

"Peter," said a voice. That was a voice I KNEW. That WAS Peter's voice! But how could this be? I was so startled that I ran back to the room full of praying people. I didn't even open the door!

"Peter's at the door! Peter's at the door!" I said breathlessly.

"WHAT?" they asked.

I told them again.

"You must be crazy! Peter's in prison. He can't be at the door."

"But I tell you, he is at the door," I said again. I was so excited!

The others talked among themselves; someone said, "Maybe she's seen an angel." I guess they thought Peter's ghost was at the door!

But meanwhile, Peter was still POUNDING on the door! So they sent me to answer it again. When the door was opened, there he was! Everyone could see it was Peter. It was really him! Everyone was astonished. We all began talking at once.

God's Answer to Prayer

Peter put his finger to his lips. He told us, "My friends, God heard your prayers for me. I was taken to prison, as you saw. A prison guard was chained to each of my hands. AND two more guards stood at my cell door. I fell asleep expecting that in the morning Herod would put me on trial— and have me put to death."

"Yes, we were afraid of the same thing. That's why we were praying! We were pleading with God to stop Herod," someone said as I hurried to get Peter some food.

"Well, God did!" Peter said cheerfully. "He sent an angel to me, right there in the prison cell. This angel touched my side and woke me up. My cell was full of light—at NIGHT! Then the angel told me to get up quickly. I didn't even have time to think before my chains just fell off. The angel told me to get my coat and follow him. And I did. We walked right past the first guard, then past the second.

"Ahead of us now was the huge iron gate into the city. *How will we get through this?* I wondered. But the gate opened for us as if an invisible hand were pushing it! I thought I must be dreaming. I thought I would wake up in the cell, still chained to the two

guards. But after I had followed the angel to the end of the street, the angel simply DISAPPEARED! Suddenly, I knew I wasn't dreaming. God had sent an angel to rescue me! God heard and answered your prayers this very night!" Peter finished.

I was so happy that Peter was safe. Then I understood. God had heard and answered our prayers! I was so amazed, I nearly dropped a dish! As soon as I had the food on the table for Peter, we all stopped right then and there to pray again. We wanted to THANK God for sending Peter safely back to us! After we visited with Peter for awhile, he quietly left for another town.

The Rest of the Rescue

Well, the next day while I was sweeping the porch, I heard that there had been a huge commotion at the prison. Everyone was talking about the missionary named Peter. No one could figure it out. This man who was chained to two guards and guarded by two more had just vanished! Bet they'll never guess how that happened!

So my day that began so terribly ended wonderfully! Even though Peter had been arrested, God wanted him to keep on being a missionary—telling others about Jesus. And when we prayed for God to rescue Peter, what a RESCUE JOB God did! I learned that day just how important it is to pray. God really hears—and He ANSWERS our prayers.

Use the questions below after telling the Bible story, during activity times or as part of Response Time.

1.
What trouble did the Christians in Jerusalem face?
(People were being killed for being Christians.
Peter was put in prison.)

2.
What could they do about it?
(Pray.)

3.
What are some things you could pray about for
(name of missionary)**?**

MISSIONARIES, NOT GODS

What it's like to be a missionary in trouble!
Acts 14:1-20

God had chosen Paul and Barnabas to be missionaries, telling the good news about Jesus. Until this time, almost all of God's family was made up of Jewish people. (Gentiles are all the people who are not Jewish.) Most Gentiles had never heard about Jesus. But now Paul and Barnabas had the job of spreading the news of Jesus to everyone, Jew and Gentile.

Of course they weren't content to just tell the people in one town about Jesus. They traveled from city to city, sharing the good news of Jesus Christ with EVERYONE! The message that God forgives anyone who asks for forgiveness of sins and believes in Jesus was big news wherever they went! Crowds came to listen—and many people became members of God's family.

But some of the religious leaders in these cities were FURIOUS at Paul and Barnabas. They forced them to leave one town. At another place, the leaders tried to KILL them!

To Lystra

Most people probably would have given up and gone home. But not Paul and Barnabas! They knew God's power would protect them. So, on they traveled.

As Paul and Barnabas reached the city of Lystra, they probably noticed the temple of the god Zeus. The people of Lystra believed in myths about gods and goddesses. They believed the gods and goddesses looked like people or animals. And they believed that Zeus, also called Jupiter, was the most powerful god. They worshiped him at this beautiful temple.

The first thing Paul and Barnabas did when they arrived in Lystra was to preach the good news about Jesus. And as usual, a large crowd gathered to hear Paul preach.

A Miracle

One man in that crowd listened carefully to every word Paul said. This man's feet were crippled. He was unable to walk—he had been crippled since the day he was born! Paul noticed this man. He saw that the man believed God's power could heal him. Paul called, "Stand up on your feet!" The man did just what Paul said! But he didn't just stand up, he JUMPED up! Then he started WALKING around! God's power healed the man right then and there. And the crowd went wild!

An Excited Crowd

The people began to talk excitedly among themselves. "The gods have come to our town disguised as these men!" they said to each other. There was an old legend that Zeus and his messenger Hermes had once come to Lystra disguised as men. The legend said that no one but an old man and his wife had welcomed them and the town had been punished!

The crowd decided that Barnabas was Zeus and that Paul—who did most of the talking—must be the messenger, Hermes. Remembering what the legend said, they didn't want to make the same mistake twice! So they rushed off to the temple of Zeus to get their priest.

Paul and Barnabas couldn't figure out WHAT was going on! But soon the whole town was marching toward Paul and Barnabas. Heading the parade was the priest of Zeus who brought wreaths and led several large oxen for a sacrifice. It became perfectly clear—these people were making a TERRIBLE mistake! They planned to WORSHIP Paul and Barnabas!

One True God

Paul and Barnabas ripped their clothes as a way of showing their sadness. They RAN into the crowd yelling, "Why are you doing this? We are just MEN, human beings like you! We came here to tell you the good news about the only living God who is the Creator of all things!"

Paul began to talk of the many proofs of a living, loving God: the rain, the crops, the seasons and the many good things that filled their lives.

"Only the one true God could create these things," Paul explained. "NOT idols—and NOT men like us!" But some people STILL wanted to believe that Paul and Barnabas were gods. Finally, Paul and Barnabas made the crowd understand that they could NOT offer a sacrifice to them.

Now about that time, some of the same people who had tried to kill Paul suddenly arrived in Lystra! They were determined to stop Paul and Barnabas from telling more people about Jesus. So they started talking to the people and tried to make them angry. Soon the people of Lystra had forgotten the miracle. They decided that the two men they had thought were gods were really troublemakers!

Finally, a furious mob stormed down the streets and grabbed Paul. They threw rocks at him until he collapsed. The crowd dragged his body outside the town, and left him alone only because they thought he was dead.

But Paul's Christian friends gathered around him and helped him back into town. The very next day Paul and Barnabas were back on the road, traveling toward the next town. Again, the power of the one true God—the same power that had made the man walk—kept Paul and Barnabas strong so they could keep on traveling and telling the good news about Jesus Christ.

Use the questions below after telling the Bible story, during activity times or as part of Response Time.

1.
Why did the people of Lystra want to worship Paul and Barnabas?
(They saw the miracle. They thought Paul and Barnabas were Zeus and Hermes.)

2.
What did the leaders who opposed Paul and Barnabas do when they got to Lystra?
(Convinced the crowds that Paul and Barnabas were really troublemakers.)

3.
What kinds of problems do (names of missionaries) **face today?**
Are they the same? different? How?
(Missionaries may be considered troublemakers and put in prison or hurt.
Missionaries may be mistaken as gods.)

4.
What would you tell a missionary who is having trouble?
(God will help you.)
What could you do to encourage a missionary?
(Pray for them. If there is something that can be done, such as sending food or money,
plan a way to do this. Send encouraging Bible verses such as Romans 8:28,38,39.)

LYDIA SHARES

How one believer shared to help the missionaries.
Acts 16:6-15,40; 17:4,12

When Jesus went back to heaven, He promised His disciples power to tell everyone the good news about Him. Not long after that, Jesus' promise came true. The Holy Spirit came. And many people began to travel around, telling others the good news about Jesus. They would go to cities and towns, telling the good news about God's Son and how people could become members of God's family. **What do you think these people who traveled around were called?** (Volunteers answer.)

Ready to Go

One of these missionaries was a man named Paul. Once, he had HATED Jesus and His followers, but now Paul loved Jesus very much. Every time he had a chance, he told other people that Jesus loves them and that Jesus died to take the punishment for all the wrong things they had ever done. (The Bible word for wrong things is "sin.") Paul also taught the people more about God and what He wants people to do to live happily with each other. Now Paul was traveling to another place so he could tell more people about Jesus. One night, while he was sleeping, he had a dream. In his dream a man said, "Please come to Macedonia (MAS-uh-DOE-nee-yuh) and help us!" So when Paul woke up, he changed his travel plans. He decided to sail for Philippi (FILL-up-pie), the capital city of Macedonia.

Ready to Hear

Now in Philippi, there lived a woman named Lydia. Lydia owned her own business—she sold purple cloth. In Bible times purple cloth was very valuable, because purple dye was VERY hard to get. Purple dye had to be gathered DROP by DROP from certain shellfish! Only the very best clothes were made from it. In fact, only kings and queens and VERY rich people could afford to buy clothes made from purple cloth.

Lydia must have made quite a lot of money selling purple cloth. She lived in a large house and had several servants. The Bible tells us that Lydia loved God. It seems that she had heard about Him from the Jewish people. Every Saturday she and some other women met on the banks of a river to pray. But Lydia didn't know about God's Son, Jesus, and His love and forgiveness.

One day while Lydia and her friends were praying, Paul and his friends joined them. **What do you think Paul wanted to tell the women when he saw them praying?** (Volunteers answer.)

Paul told them about Jesus. He explained to them that Jesus is God's Son. He told them how Jesus had died on the cross so their sins could be forgiven. Then Paul explained how Jesus had risen from the dead and gone back to heaven.

Ready to Receive

Lydia listened carefully to everything Paul said. Even though Lydia loved God, this was the FIRST time she had heard about Jesus. As Lydia listened to Paul, God helped her understand. God's Spirit helped her to believe what Paul was saying. Lydia asked Jesus to forgive her sins. She was baptized to show that she had become a member of God's family. (Baptism uses water to show that God has made a person clean from the wrong things he or she has done.) When Lydia's family and helpers heard about Jesus, they also believed the things Paul told them. They believed Jesus is God's Son. They asked Jesus to forgive their sins. And they were baptized.

There must have been quite a celebration, for now they were part of God's family, too! Everyone in Lydia's household was glad that Paul had told them about Jesus!

Ready to Share

Lydia was very thankful for God's love and for sending Paul to tell her about Jesus. She wanted to help Paul. She wanted other people to be able to learn about Jesus, too.

"Paul," she said, "while you and your friends are teaching here in Philippi, please come and stay in my home."

So Paul and his friends stayed at Lydia's house. Every day, they talked to people in Philippi, telling more and more people about Jesus. More and more people became members of God's family! Because Lydia was willing to give her house and food to help Paul and his friends, they had more time to keep telling people about Jesus.

Then Lydia learned from Paul that it was important for people who loved Jesus to meet together. So she began to invite the people who loved Jesus to come to her house. At Lydia's house, they sang and prayed together. And they all kept learning more about Jesus from Paul and his friends. The people in the church at Lydia's house told their friends about Jesus, too.

Because Lydia was now part of God's family, she wanted to share. She used her money to buy food for the missionaries, Paul and his friends. She shared her house so Paul and his friends had a place to stay. She also shared her house with the people who loved Jesus by giving them a place to meet. By sharing what she had, she helped many people hear the good news about God's Son, Jesus.

Use the questions below after telling the Bible story, during activity times or as part of Response Time.

1.
What are ways that Lydia and her household showed their love for God?
(They shared their home and food.)

2.
What ways do people in your church show their love for God?
(They pray and give money to help support missionaries.)
How does your family show love?
(Sends packages to missionaries. Writes to missionaries.
Gives money to a missionary offering.
Provides a place for missionaries to stay when in this country.)

3.
Name some ways that you can help and encourage missionaries.
(Welcome them when they come home.
Help with sending them packages, writing them letters and giving money for their support.)

TEACHING A TEACHER

One helps another who helps another...

Acts 18:1-4,18-28

Aquila (Ah-KWIL-uh) and his wife Priscilla (pris-SIL-uh) were Jewish people. They were both born and raised in Rome. But Claudius, the Roman ruler, had commanded that all Jewish people had to leave Rome. So, Priscilla and Aquila had to move. It must have been hard to leave their home. But when they moved quite far away, to Corinth, they couldn't have guessed what exciting things were going to happen to them!

New Home, New Friends

Aquila and Priscilla earned their living by making tents. One day a Jewish man named Paul, who was also a tentmaker, came to talk to them. Priscilla and Aquila got to know Paul. They invited Paul to stay with them. He helped them make tents, but he did much, much more besides!

Paul was a missionary. He knew all about Jesus. He knew that Jesus had died for the sins, or wrong things, people have done. Paul also knew that Jesus is alive. He knew that anyone could know Jesus now and live with Him forever. Besides that, Paul knew how much Jesus wanted everyone to know about Him. So, once a week when the Jewish people went to their synagogue, Paul came and told them all about Jesus.

What do you think they learned from Paul? (Volunteers give ideas.)

Priscilla and Aquila learned all about Jesus from Paul. In fact, many of the people in Corinth who heard Paul teach about Jesus became members of God's family, and God's family in Corinth grew and grew! Priscilla and Aquila were part of that church where Paul preached and taught. And the three of them kept on making tents, too. But one day, it was time for Paul to move on. He had stayed in Corinth for some time, but now it was time to go to Ephesus (EF-uh-sus).

Guess who decided to go with Paul? (Volunteers answer.)

Another Move

Priscilla and Aquila sailed with Paul to Ephesus. Paul preached in the synagogue and taught many Jewish people about Jesus. "Paul, please stay! Teach us more," the Jewish believers pleaded.

"I must go on and tell others about Jesus. That's the job God has given me to do. But if God wants me to, I will come and visit you again," Paul said. But this time, Priscilla and Aquila didn't go with Paul. They stayed in Ephesus so they could teach and help the other believers there. The time had come for Priscilla and Aquila to become missionaries in Ephesus!

Teaching a Teacher

One day a Jewish man from Alexandria (a city in Egypt) came to Ephesus. His name was Apollos and he had spent a lot of time studying the oldest part of the Bible. He knew a great deal about it. He taught the other believers all that he knew. But as they listened, Priscilla and Aquila found out that Apollos didn't know about Jesus at all. Apollos only knew about the message John the Baptist had preached. Apollos knew that the Messiah would come, but he did not know Jesus was the Messiah John the Baptist had said would come.

What do you think Priscilla and Aquila did when they found out what Apollos didn't know? (Volunteers answer.)

Aquila and Priscilla knew it was important to teach this teacher. So they invited Apollos to their home. They taught Apollos that the promised Messiah was Jesus, who had been crucified and lives again. Now he knew the whole story of the good news! And Apollos could teach all of the good news about Jesus.

One day, it was time for Apollos to move on, too. Apollos wanted to go to Achaia (uh-KAY-uh) to encourage the believers there. So Aquila and Priscilla and the other believers in Ephesus wrote to the believers in Achaia and asked them to welcome Apollos to their town and to their group.

Apollos was a great help to the believers in Achaia. Paul had taught Aquila and Priscilla. Then Aquila and Priscilla had taught this teacher, Apollos, so he could become a missionary, too—telling the whole story of the good news about Jesus.

Use the questions below after telling the Bible story, during activity times or as part of Response Time.

1.

Who helped Priscilla and Aquila learn about Jesus?
(Paul.)
Who did Priscilla and Aquila teach about Jesus?
(Apollos and others in Ephesus.)

2.

What are some ways missionaries encourage and help others today?
(Translate the Bible into the language of the people.
Provide teachers, money, materials and various kinds of help to churches that need these kinds of help.)
Is it the same today as in Paul's time?
(Missionaries still help others learn how to teach about Jesus.)
What is different?
(Bibles are available in many languages so that many people can learn all about Jesus from the Bible.)

3.

What are some ways you can give help and encouragement to (name of missionary)**?**
(Write letters. Send gifts. Pray.)

ALWAYS A MISSIONARY

How Paul the missionary persevered through trouble.
Acts 27

Trouble on the Way

Paul was a missionary. No matter what, he was going to tell people the good news about Jesus! But now Paul was also a prisoner. He had been telling so many people about Jesus that it made some leaders angry. Those leaders had Paul arrested. But even then Paul was a missionary! As a prisoner, he had talked with several Roman rulers, telling them about Jesus. The rulers agreed there was no reason to keep Paul in prison. But each of them passed off the decision about freeing Paul to someone else! Finally, Paul had asked to talk to the mightiest Roman ruler of them all—the emperor. To Paul, being a prisoner and talking to rulers were just part of being a missionary!

Tough Travel

For Paul, being a missionary also meant traveling. To get to Rome, where the emperor was, he would travel a long way by ship, which could take months. And the weather could make sailing in a boat very dangerous! But for Paul, that was all part of being a missionary!

Who knows? Perhaps I can tell many people on this ship about Jesus! Paul may have thought. Soon they were off! But when the ship set sail, the howling wind nearly blew it off course. Finally, the travelers arrived at another port, where they boarded a large Egyptian ship. It was sailing for Italy—across the Mediterranean Sea where the emperor lived.

Storm at Sea

The ship buzzed with activity as bags, boxes and 276 people were loaded. The sailing had already been rough and difficult. But now things got worse! It was the season when the winds were beginning to blow their hardest. Although Paul warned that they would have a great deal of trouble, the captain of the ship decided to sail anyway.

At first the sea was calm, with a gentle wind. But THEN the winds began to blow HARDER. Waves grew larger and LARGER. The wind and waves tossed the ship from side to side like a toy. The ship creaked and groaned as if it would break into pieces! For days and days the storm raged. The sailors knew their ship could not hold together if the storm didn't let up SOON.

"The ship is too heavy!" shouted the captain. "Throw out everything that we don't need to survive!" But in spite of all that, the terrible storm raged on. The passengers huddled together in terror.

"We're all going to die!" cried the sailors in despair. "Nothing can save us!"

Paul's Good News

In the middle of all these TERRIFIED people, Paul stood up. "Cheer up!" he said. "I have good news. Last night, an angel of the true God stood beside me. The angel told me not to be afraid. 'Not one of the people on this ship will be hurt,' the angel said. I know God. And I'm sure it will happen just as the angel said."

Paul the missionary just couldn't keep good news to himself, even in the middle of the most HORRIBLE storm! God knew about the storm. And God had promised they would be safe! The passengers and crew were encouraged when they heard Paul's news.

But for two more weeks the storm did not let up. Then at midnight on the fourteenth day, the sailors discovered that they were sailing in shallow water. Now they were really afraid! If the ship hit a rock or sandbar, it would break apart in the storm.

Just before daylight, Paul again encouraged his miserable, frightened shipmates. "Please eat. You will soon need all your strength. Don't be so worried!" Paul added. "Every one of you will make it to shore alive."

Taking some bread in his hand, Paul thanked God for the food. Soon all the passengers were eating—and feeling more hopeful!

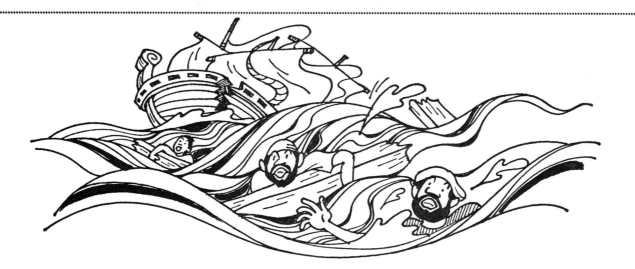

Safe on Shore

At dawn, the passengers and sailors on board the ship looked anxiously toward the sandy beach ahead. "Captain," the sailors called, "we're not sure we can make it!"

The captain shouted, "We've got to try. Cut the anchors. Raise the sail and head for shore!"

The sailors obeyed. Then the front of the ship hit a sandbar and stuck fast! Waves crashed against it, and it began to break apart.

"We'd better KILL all the prisoners," said the soldiers. "Otherwise they'll swim ashore and escape!"

But the army commander said, "No! Anyone who can swim—jump overboard and swim for land! Otherwise, grab some wood and float to shore!" One by one the ship's passengers, sailors and prisoners all jumped in. They swam and struggled through the water, with the memory of Paul's encouraging words to help them keep going!

As they struggled onto the beach, they looked back. The ship was in pieces! But NO ONE had been lost! And there on that island, Paul began to gather firewood to help keep everyone warm. He kept right on telling people about the good news of Jesus. Whether he was a prisoner, in a storm or shipwrecked on an island—trouble was all just part of being a missionary for Paul!

Use the questions below after telling the Bible story, during activity times or as part of Response Time.

1.
What things did Paul face that could have made him want to give up?
(He was a prisoner. He had to travel a very long way. He was in a storm and a shipwreck.)

2.
What did Paul do about his troubles?
(Prayed. Continued to be kind and tell others about Jesus, no matter what happened to him.)

3.
What kinds of troubles do (name of missionaries) **face?**
What can you do to encourage missionaries?
(Pray for them. Write letters to encourage them. Give money or needed items.
Welcome them to your home when they come to visit.)

GROWING A CHURCH

Timothy tells about his job as gardener, er... pastor.
1 Timothy 1—4; 2 Timothy 1:4—4:8

What does a garden need to grow? (Prepared soil. Seed. Sunshine. Water. Someone to pull out the weeds.)

My name is Timothy. I live in Ephesus (EF-uh-sus). It's not exactly a garden spot; it's a big city. But let me tell you about the gardening job I was asked to do! When Paul the missionary left for Macedonia, he left me here as the chief gardener. Now, I'm not exactly growing plants. No, I'm in charge of growing the whole CHURCH in Ephesus! Even though I'm not very old, Paul believed that growing this church was God's assignment for me. AND he believed that I could do it. *But how?* I kept asking myself.

Preparing the Soil

Paul wrote me a letter about how to get started. There were some people who were teaching wrong things. It was my job to help them stop teaching these wrong things and start paying attention to having a pure heart and real faith. Paul also said we all needed to pray about everything. So I prayed a lot. And God answered!

Planting Seeds

What do you think Paul told me was most important to tell the people in the church? (Volunteers answer.) The only way to grow a healthy church is from good seed! Now Paul had planted lots of the good seed of God's Word when he was in Ephesus. But now I had to keep on planting good seed—telling people about Jesus and how much He loves them.

So I told people the good news about Jesus—how Jesus died for all the wrong things we do, and that He lives again. I told them that believing in Jesus, not praying to idols, was the only way to know God and that anyone could know God and become a part of His family. All anyone had to do was believe what Jesus had done, tell God he or she was sorry for the wrong things he or she had done and ask to become

God's child. When the good seed of God's Word was planted, more and more people began to understand God's wonderful love for them. They became members of God's family—part of our church and God's garden! And they began to grow! Oh, they didn't get taller. They didn't turn green. But by God's Spirit in them, each of them grew on the inside—they were growing in knowing Jesus!

More Gardeners

Before long, there were many people in the church. Like a garden full of different plants, they had many different needs. And I needed help! That's why Paul wrote to me again. He told me how to choose leaders to help me take care of the church the way good gardeners care for their plants. **What kind of people would be good leaders?** (People who obeyed God in every part of their lives.) My new gardeners were a BIG help! Now I didn't feel like I was all alone! God helped me again—by bringing other people to help!

Tending Plants

In my "church-garden" full of different plants, God's Word was like sunshine and water! I read the Bible to the people (people in Bible-times didn't have Bibles of their own). And I preached and taught everything that I had learned about God. I was REALLY glad that I had listened to Paul, my grandmother and mother when they taught the Bible to me. That made me ready to teach others. Just like in any garden, sometimes there were bugs and weeds. Some people in the church still believed in idols. That really "bugged" me! And they began telling others to pray to idols! Paul wrote to me, "Tell the people that praying to idols is wrong. Idols can't hear and answer prayer." So I had to tell them this was wrong. It wasn't easy, but God helped me!

Later, there was a really BIG problem. Some "big

weeds" grew up and tried to choke out my garden! The "big weeds" were people who said God had told them to be teachers. And they taught that it wasn't good to marry and that some food was a sin to eat—and all kinds of other things that weren't from God's Word! So I had to tell them to stop teaching. I also had to tell all the people that these people had been teaching wrong things. **How do you think I felt about having to do this?** (Scared!) But if I didn't, my people would be confused about God. Once again, God helped me to do what He wanted me to do.

Now those false teachers didn't like being corrected by me—especially since I was a lot younger than they were. But Paul reminded me that it was GOD'S idea for me to be the main gardener of this church of His.

Paul wrote, "Don't let any of them look down at you just because you are younger than they are. Live as an example to others." So God helped me stand up straight and continue to teach God's Word, even when some people didn't like it.

The Church Grows

I loved the church that God had given me to take care of. It was like a beautiful garden to me! Sure, there were weeds—and bugs and slugs, too! But I prayed every day for the leaders and the people. I tried my best to teach God's ways and live them, too. God gave me so much love for the people in my church, I loved them like my own family! And God grew that church He planted, stronger and more loving every day!

Use the questions below after telling the Bible story, during activity times or as part of Response Time.

1.
What did Timothy do to help God's church grow?
(Prayed. Told people about Jesus. Taught God's Word.
Corrected wrong teaching. Lived as an example. Showed love.)

2.
What are ways missionaries (and others) **help the church grow today?**
How are these ways the same as in Timothy's day?
(Pray. Tell people about Jesus. Correct wrong teaching.
They live as an example and show love.)
How are they different?
(There are more church buildings now.
Travel and communication is easier now.
Many more people now have Bibles to study.)

3.
What are some ways you can help your church grow?
(Pray. Be friendly to the people who attend your church.
Invite others to your church.)

CRAFTS

Crafts are a wonderful way to involve the whole child in learning!

A child's **imagination** will be sparked. Weaving on a loom or creating a display about missions encourages the child to imagine and thus identify with life in other countries and cultures.

A child's **mind** will be working rapidly, absorbing new information and understanding new ways of doing things. Some children think more clearly when they are doing something than when they are sitting still!

A child's **hands** will be occupied; more than that, he or she will be making an object to keep or to share. Because children are concrete thinkers, making a tangible reminder can help them better remember the lesson.

A child's **creativity** will soar while exploring the ways he or she can make the item uniquely his or hers, by adding details unique to that other culture or decorating the item differently from anyone else's.

Crafts around the World will introduce children to a different culture through the making of an item from that culture.

Missions Crafts will provide opportunities for children to think about missions and missionaries in a variety of ways, whether comparing and contrasting missions then and now or exploring ways to pray for specific missionaries.

Service Projects are practical activities children can do to help and encourage missionaries or raise funds for a missions project.

African Kitchen Fan

ALL AGES WITH HELP; THIRD GRADE AND UP ALONE / 20-30 MINUTES

MATERIALS: World map, brown chenille wires (eight for each child), raffia (available at craft stores), scissors, 12-inch (30-cm) sticks or dowels about ½ inch (1.25 cm) in diameter, measuring stick.

PREPARATION: For each child, cut raffia into 3-4 ft. (1-1.25 m) lengths and cut sticks into 12-inch (30-cm) lengths for handles.

PROCEDURE: Display a world map. **Who can show me where Africa is? What missionaries do we know there?** Volunteers tell. **Sometimes people make fans to keep themselves cool. But in Africa, fans are used another way, too—in the kitchen. Many people cook over wood fires and the boys and girls must add wood to the fires and keep the fires going. They use their fans to fan the flames and keep the fires hot. Their fans are usually round with long handles. We're going to make kitchen fans today.**

TO MAKE AN AFRICAN KITCHEN FAN, FOLLOW THESE STEPS:

Step 1: Take six chenille wires. Cut one wire in half. Hold the other five wires together and wrap one half-wire around center of the bundle once (sketch a).

Step 2: Spread the wires to create eleven spokes (sketch b).

Step 3: Wind the end of a length of raffia around the center of chenille-wire bundle several times to secure. Then weave raffia over and under the chenille-wire spokes (sketch c).

Step 4: To keep weaving, add another length of raffia. Lay end of old length next to end of new piece and knot. Tuck knot to back side of fan.

Step 5: When raffia is woven to about 1½ inches (3.25-cm) from the outer ends of the chenille wires, tie end of raffia to a chenille-wire spoke, then bend remaining chenille wire ends over and under raffia (sketch d). (More raffia may be wound through outer edge in whip-stitch fashion to make fan more sturdy.)

Step 6: Attach stick handle to back of fan by laying stick at center of fan back, on top of one spoke. Loop two chenille wires back and forth through the fan front along the spoke (sketch e). Twist wires tightly to secure handle.

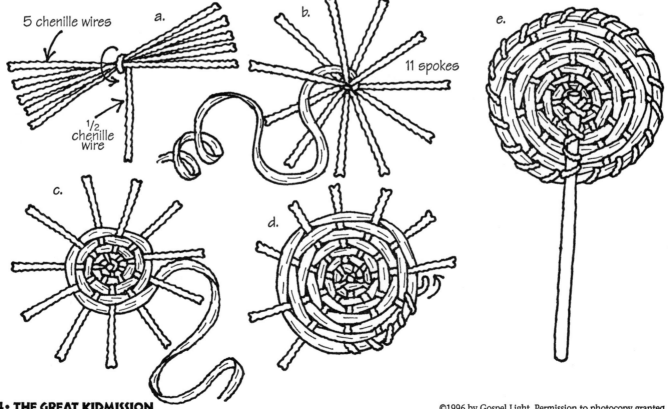

5 chenille wires

a.

½ chenille wire

b.

11 spokes

e.

c.

d.

African Mud Cloth

YOUNGER ELEMENTARY WITH HELP; OLDER ALONE / 30-40 MINUTES

MATERIALS: World map, muslin or cotton cloth (old bed sheets work well), measuring stick, mud, wire mesh strainer, blue tempera paint, small coffee can with plastic lid, small containers, spoon, pencil, painting tools (paintbrushes, wooden tongue depressors, small tree branches, etc.).

PREPARATION: Cut fabric into 15-inch (37.5-cm) squares, one for each child. Then prepare the mud. You will need 1 cup of filtered mud for every four to six children.

At the sink, place a strainer over a coffee can. Put a handful of mud in the strainer. Run water over the mud, stirring with finger or stick.

Throw away debris left in the strainer and let mud sink to the bottom of the can, leaving a layer of water on top.

Pour off water and repeat the straining process until enough mud is prepared.

PROCEDURE: Show world map. Point out Ivory Coast area of West Africa. **The Korhogo people of the Ivory Coast paint designs with mud on hand-woven cotton cloth. They prepare the mud especially for decorating their cloth. We're going to decorate some cloth like they do.**

TO MAKE THE MUD CLOTH, FOLLOW THESE STEPS:

Step 1: Add ¼ cup blue tempera paint to 1 cup cleaned mud in can and stir well.

Step 2: Draw a design in pencil on the cotton cloth. (See sketches for ideas.)

Step 3: Place a small amount of mud paint in a container and paint! Use painting tools to paint.

Put paint in covered container to store it. If mud paint dries out, add a little water. This project can be extended over several days, depending on how much cloth is being decorated.

Step 4: Let mud paint dry (20-30 minutes or overnight).

ENRICHMENT IDEA: Make your own African clothing. Bring several cans of filtered mud paint and old white cotton sheets. Give each child 1-2 yards (1-2 m) of fabric to paint (depending on size of child). When fabric is painted and dry, use as wrap-around clothing or sarong.

Turtle design

Small animal design

African Rain Stick

OLDER ELEMENTARY / 30-40 MINUTES

MATERIALS: World map, cardboard tube from paper towel roll, wire nails (available at craft or hardware stores), Con-Tact® paper, measuring stick, scissors, glue, thin cardboard, rubber bands, small objects (tiny glass beads, shells, rice, etc.).

PREPARATION: Cut Con-Tact® paper into 6x12-inch (15x30-cm) rectangles.

PROCEDURE: Show map of the world. Talk about missionaries who work in Africa. **In Africa, rain sticks are used to accompany songs. In some African churches, rain sticks accompany worship songs.**

**TO MAKE A RAIN STICK,
FOLLOW THESE STEPS:**

Step 1: Press wire nails through the spiral slot on the cardboard tube, ½ inch apart (sketch a). Continue down the entire length of the tube.

Step 2: Cut two cardboard circles, 3 inches (7.5 cm) in diameter. Slit as shown in sketch b.

Step 3: Cover one end of the tube with a circle, fold down the slits, and glue ends down. Secure ends with a rubber band while drying (sketch c).

Step 4: Fill the tube about one-tenth full with tiny beads, shells, rice, etc.; then repeat Step 3 to cover other end of tube. When ends have dried, remove rubber bands.

Step 5: Cover tube with Con-Tact® paper.

To play, hold tube at a sixty-degree angle and tilt gently from end to end until desired "rain sounds" are heard.

ENRICHMENT IDEA: Add potato prints to rain sticks: Instead of Con-Tact® paper, bring art tape (or strips of colored construction paper and masking tape), small potatoes, paring knives and black tempera paint. Cut a potato in half and cut shapes into the flat surface of the potato. Dip the potato into black tempera paint, then stamp repeatedly onto art tape. Wrap art tape around the tube. Any leftover art tape can be made into headbands or wrist and ankle bracelets.

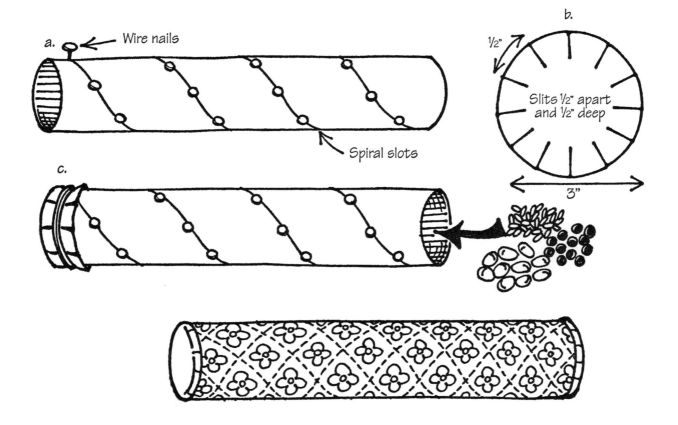

a. Wire nails
Spiral slots

b. ½"
Slits ½" apart and ½" deep
3"

c.

African Rattle

ALL AGES / 15-20 MINUTES

MATERIALS: Colorful construction paper, dried beans or pebbles, masking tape, markers, scissors, glue, sandpaper. For each child—a one-liter plastic soda bottle and one 12-inch (30-cm) dowel or stick (sized to fit inside soda bottle opening).

PREPARATION: Remove the labels from the soda bottles.

PROCEDURE: Name one or two missionary families who work in Africa. **In Africa, many people make rattles out of gourds. What is a gourd?** (A rounded, hollow squash-like vegetable.) **People in Africa and all over the world grow gourds in their gardens. They use gourds to make bottles, bowls, dishes and toys. How many of you grow gourds at home? We are going to make rattles that may look like they're made from gourds. But we'll use soda bottles for our gourds!**

TO MAKE THE RATTLE, FOLLOW THESE STEPS:

Step 1: Sand sticks to remove rough edges.

Step 2: Decorate soda bottles by drawing designs on sheets of construction paper and then gluing paper around bottles (sketch a). Or apply glue to an area of the bottle, then add cut or torn paper pieces to bottle to create a design (sketch b). Let dry.

Step 3: Drop a small handful of dried beans or pebbles into bottle opening (sketch c).

Step 4: Apply glue around inside of bottle opening and insert dowel into opening. Tap dowel in firmly. Let glue dry. Then secure handle by wrapping the area with masking tape (sketch d).

ENRICHMENT IDEAS: Glue yarn, beads, etc. to bottle for decoration.

If dried gourds are available, use them. Paint gourds with acrylic paints or cover with colored tissue paper dipped in a half-glue, half-water mixture.

a.

Sheet of decorated construction paper

b.

c.

d.

Glue

Masking tape

Australian Sheep Farm

ALL AGES / 20-30 MINUTES

MATERIALS: World map, glue, cotton balls, scissors, colored construction paper (green, brown, gray, white, blue, black).

PREPARATION: Make a sample according to directions below.

PROCEDURE: Show a map of the world. **How many continents are there? Where is the continent of Australia? What people do we know who live there? Do you know what animals live in Australia? One kind of animal that lives there is the sheep. Australia is famous for raising sheep for meat and for wool. Today we're going to make collages that look like sheep farms. When we see our collages at** home, **they will help us remember to pray for our missionaries in Australia.**

TO MAKE A SHEEP FARM COLLAGE, FOLLOW THESE STEPS:

Step 1: Use a sheet of green paper as the bottom sheet for your collage. Cut or tear pieces of brown and gray paper and glue them onto the green paper wherever you'd like to make stone walls.

Step 2: Tear cotton balls apart and make as many small balls as you'd like to represent sheep. Glue these to your collage.

Step 3: As you imagine your sheep farm, add whatever details you like—trees, water, perhaps a shepherd and a wolf or two.

Green construction paper

Chinese Streamers

EARLY ELEMENTARY / 15 MINUTES

MATERIALS: World map, crepe paper streamers in a variety of bright colors, string, foil star stickers, transparent tape, scissors, measuring stick. For each child—one large plastic or wooden thread spool.

PREPARATION: Remove labels from spools. Cut crepe paper into 1-yard (.9-m) lengths—three different colors for each child. Cut string into 18-inch (45-cm) lengths—one for each child.

PROCEDURE: Show China on a map. **What missionaries do we know who work in China? In China, children often wave streamers during parades. Today we're going to make our own Chinese streamers.**

TO MAKE CHINESE STREAMERS, FOLLOW THESE STEPS:

Step 1: Fold one end of streamer into a point (sketch a). Repeat for other two streamers.

Step 2: Tape points of streamers onto spool (sketch b). Decorate with star stickers.

Step 3: Thread string through center of spool. With teacher's help, tie a knot to secure the string (sketch b).

Step 4: Hold spool by string and wave in the air. **What shapes can you make by waving your streamers in the air? Can you make a circle?** Wind streamers around spool when not in use.

ENRICHMENT IDEA: Instead of holding spool by string, make a long handle by inserting and gluing a dowel into center of spool (sketch c).

a.

b. Spool

Tape

c.

Enrichment Idea

Dowel

Egyptian Paper Beads

YOUNGER ELEMENTARY WITH HELP; OLDER ALONE / 20-30 MINUTES

MATERIALS: World map, brightly-colored magazine pages, small paintbrushes, glue, scissors, yarn, measuring stick; optional—metal washers, large buttons, macaroni.

PREPARATION: Cut yarn into 15-inch (37.5-cm) lengths, one for each child.

PROCEDURE: Show world map. **Who can show me the location of Egypt? What missionaries do we know who work there? The people of Egypt have been making beads for thousands of years. They wore wide collars of beads. Today, many Middle Eastern and African peoples wear many strings of beads and also sew beads onto their bags and clothing. We are going to make beads like the Egyptians. But our beads will be made from paper.**

**TO MAKE THE BEADS,
FOLLOW THESE STEPS:**

Step 1: Cut magazine pages into 1-inch (2.5-cm) strips (to make long beads) or into long triangles 1-inch (2.5-cm) wide at base (to make rounded beads).

Step 2: Squeeze glue on one side of each strip.

Step 3: Fold the end of the strip over. Lay the handle of a paintbrush on it. Lay folded end of the paper strip over the handle and press down (sketch a). (The glue will hold the paper down.) Place both hands on either end of the brush handle and roll gently to end of paper as shown (sketch b). Gently pull the brush handle out, to leave room for the yarn to be inserted. Repeat process to make desired number of beads.

Step 4: Let beads dry. Dip each end of the piece of yarn into a little glue and let it dry.

Step 5: String the finished beads onto the yarn. Optional: String metal washers, large buttons or macaroni between each paper bead to make jewelry more interesting (sketch c).

Enrichment Idea: Make many bead strands of different lengths and wear them together.

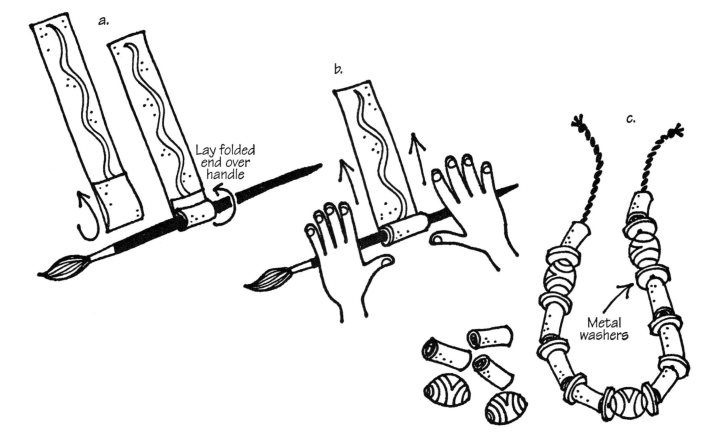

a.

Lay folded end over handle

b.

c.

Metal washers

Indian Palm Puppet

OLDER ELEMENTARY / 20-30 MINUTES

MATERIALS: World map, Indian Palm Puppet Patterns, black markers, pencils, measuring stick, masking tape, scissors, hole punch, white poster board; for each child—a drinking straw, four paper fasteners.

PREPARATION: Photocopy one set of patterns for each child. Cut three 3x8-inch (7.5x20-cm) poster board pieces for each child (sketch a).

PROCEDURE: Show world map. Talk about missionaries who work in India and the kinds of work they are doing. **In India, people shape dried fronds from palm trees into a puppet that is placed on a stick. The puppet's stick is rolled between the palms of the hands to make its arms and legs jump out as it twirls. It is called a "palm" puppet for those two reasons.**

**TO MAKE THE PUPPET,
FOLLOW THESE STEPS:**

Step 1: Cut out puppet patterns.

Step 2: Taking three 3x8-inch (7.5x20-cm) poster board pieces, fold one piece in half. Place the head/body pattern onto the fold of the cardboard and trace it. Then trace pattern on the other side of the cardboard (sketch b).

Step 3: Trace the arm pattern and leg pattern two times each on the two remaining pieces. Mark circles for fasteners on each piece.

Step 4: Cut out puppet body, arms and legs.

Step 5: Punch holes where marked, then decorate the puppet parts with black marker. (Make the same face and body design on both sides of the head/body piece as in sketch c.)

Step 6: Tape top of straw onto inside of body (sketch d), then fold over the head/body piece.

Step 7: Slip each arm between the two pieces of cardboard at shoulders; fasten loosely with paper fasteners, then fasten legs in lower holes (sketch e) so arms and legs move freely.

To make puppet dance, roll straw between palms of hands (sketch f).

ENRICHMENT IDEA: Glue yarn hair and fabric-scrap clothing to puppets.

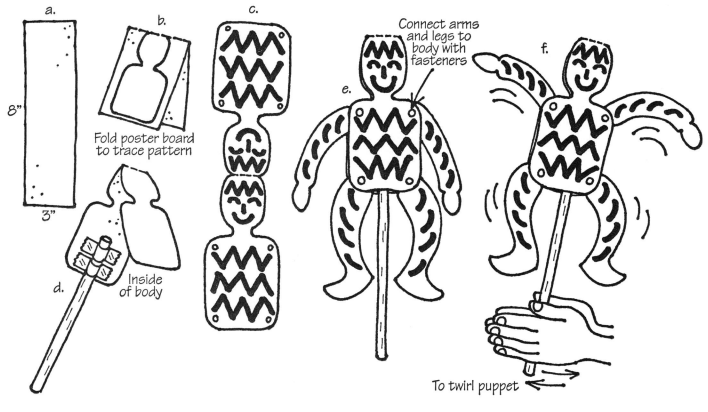

a.

8"

3"

Fold poster board
to trace pattern

d. Inside
of body

c.

Connect arms
and legs to
body with
fasteners

e.

f.

To twirl puppet

Indian Palm Puppet Patterns

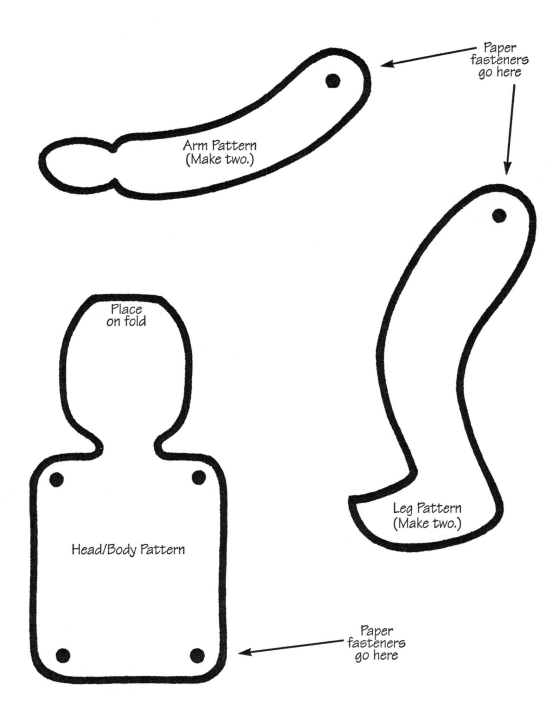

Paper fasteners go here

Arm Pattern
(Make two.)

Place on fold

Head/Body Pattern

Leg Pattern
(Make two.)

Paper fasteners go here

Indian Ring-the-Stick Game

ALL AGES / 20-30 MINUTES

MATERIALS: World map, toilet paper or paper towel tubes, tempera paint, paintbrushes, shallow containers, cotton string, Con-Tact® paper in colorful patterns, hole punch, masking tape, scissors, measuring stick, newspaper. For each child—one unsharpened pencil.

PREPARATION: Cut cardboard tubes into 1-inch (2.5-cm) widths—two for each child. Cut string into 30-inch (75-cm) lengths—one for each child. Cut Con-Tact® paper into ½x20-inch (1.25x50-cm) strips—one for each child. Cover work area with newspaper. Pour paint into shallow containers.

PROCEDURE: Show India on a world map. **What missionaries do we know who live in India? In India, children make and play a ring-the-stick game. Today we're going to make a game like the one they play.**

TO MAKE THE GAME, FOLLOW THESE STEPS:

Step 1: Cut open two cardboard tube pieces (sketch a).

Step 2: Use masking tape to join the two pieces together to make a larger ring (sketch b).

Step 3: Punch a hole in the ring and paint the outside of the ring. Let it dry.

Step 4: Peel end of backing from Con-Tact® paper strip. Holding one end of string near bottom of pencil, spiral paper strip tightly around length of pencil to secure string (sketch c).

Step 5: When paint dries, tie loose end of string through hole in ring. Hold pencil with one hand and toss ring in the air, trying to catch it on the stick.

SIMPLIFICATION IDEA: Use a wooden ring (available at most craft stores) instead of making one from cardboard tube. Instead of painting ring, decorate with markers or cover with adhesive-backed paper.

a. Cut open

b.

c. 30" string / Con-Tact® paper / Backing

Japanese Fan

ALL AGES / 15-20 MINUTES

MATERIALS: World map, Japanese Fan Pattern, light-colored poster board, scrap paper, one large wooden tongue depressor for each child, pencil, markers, scissors, heavy-duty stapler, measuring stick.

PREPARATION: Cut poster board into 7-inch (17.5-cm) squares, one for each child. Photocopy one pattern for each child.

PROCEDURE: Show world map. **Who can tell me where Japan is? What missionaries do we know who live there? The Japanese people fan themselves with paper fans called uchiwa** (OO-chee-wah), **made of split bamboo and washi** (WASH-ee), **Japanese paper. They stencil designs on their fans to decorate them. We can keep cool with our own uchiwa.**

TO MAKE THE FAN, FOLLOW THESE STEPS:

Step 1: Cut out pattern; trace it onto the poster board.

Step 2: Cut out fan.

Step 3: Use photocopied pattern or scrap paper to plan a design.

Step 4: Decorate poster board fan with markers as desired.

Step 5: Staple the tongue depressor to the fan (see sketch).

ENRICHMENT IDEA: Purchase or make stencils. Color over stencils with markers or paint with tempera paints, using brushes or sponges.

SIMPLIFICATION IDEA: Photocopy one Japanese Fan Pattern for each child. Child decorates pattern, cuts it out and glues it to poster board.

Staple tongue depressor here

Shapes for decorating fans

Japanese Fan Pattern

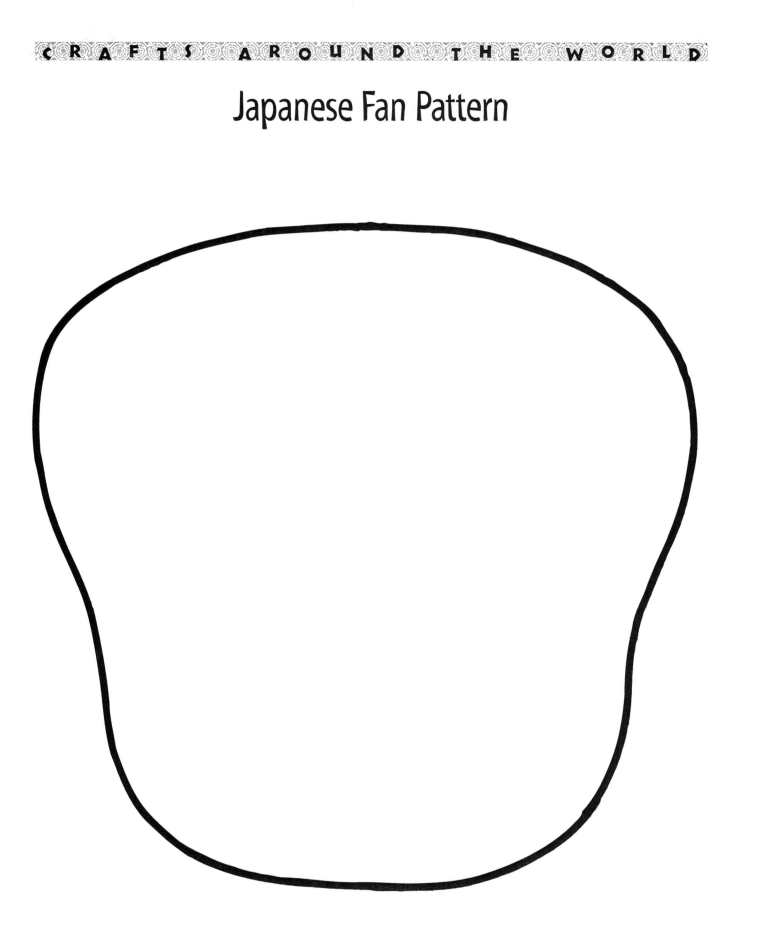

Japanese Kokeshi Doll

YOUNGER ELEMENTARY / 15-20 MINUTES

MATERIALS: World map, Japanese Kokeshi (ko-KESH-ee) Doll Kimono Pattern, cardboard toilet paper tubes, 5x7-inch (12.5x15-cm) pieces of origami (or-ih-GAH-mee) paper or wrapping paper in several patterns, tissue paper, glue, fine-tip markers, yarn, pencil, scissors, measuring stick.

PREPARATION: Photocopy one pattern for each child. Cut yarn into 6-inch (15-cm) lengths, one for each child.

PROCEDURE: Show world map. Invite volunteers to point to Japan and tell something they know about the country. **Children all over the world play with dolls. In Japan, one type of doll is called a kokeshi doll. It is made of a long, round piece of wood with a round wooden head. Kokeshi dolls have no arms or legs. Their faces, hair and clothing are all painted on. We're going to make dolls like these.**

TO MAKE A KOKESHI DOLL, FOLLOW THESE STEPS:

Step 1: Trace kimono (kee-MOH-no) pattern onto origami paper. Cut out kimono shape and apply glue around inside edges of paper. Cover tube with paper (sketch a).

Step 2: Trace and cut an obi (OOH-bee) from contrasting paper, using pattern. Glue it around doll (sketch b).

Step 3: Cut length of yarn and tie it around the doll's obi.

Step 4: Make a tightly-packed tissue-paper ball about 2 inches (5 cm) across. Then take a sheet of tissue paper and cover the ball, twisting loose paper below the ball (sketches c, d).

Step 5: Smooth tissue paper to make face area, then draw the doll's face and hair (sketch d).

Step 6: Apply glue around inside edge of cardboard tube, then insert twisted tail of tissue paper into tube, pulling tail gently through the bottom of tube until head fits snugly on top of tube. Cut off excess tail at bottom of tube (sketch e). Let dry.

ENRICHMENT IDEA: Use the photocopied pattern for the kimono. Invite children to design and draw their own "fabric" for doll's kimono.

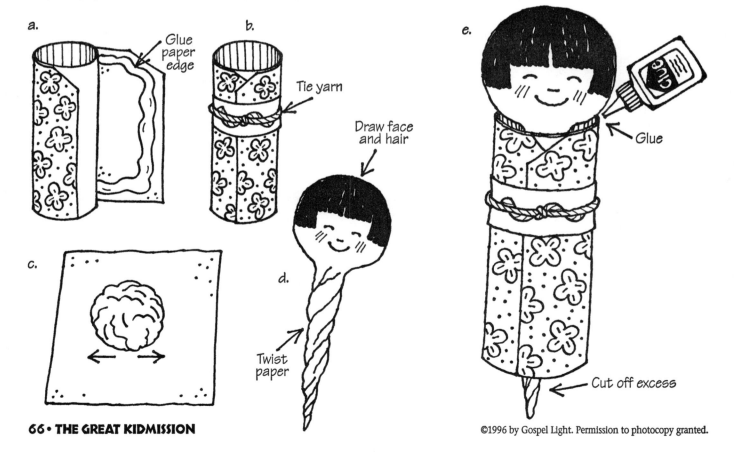

a. Glue paper edge

b. Tie yarn

Draw face and hair

c.

d. Twist paper

e. Glue

Cut off excess

Japanese Kokeshi Doll Pattern

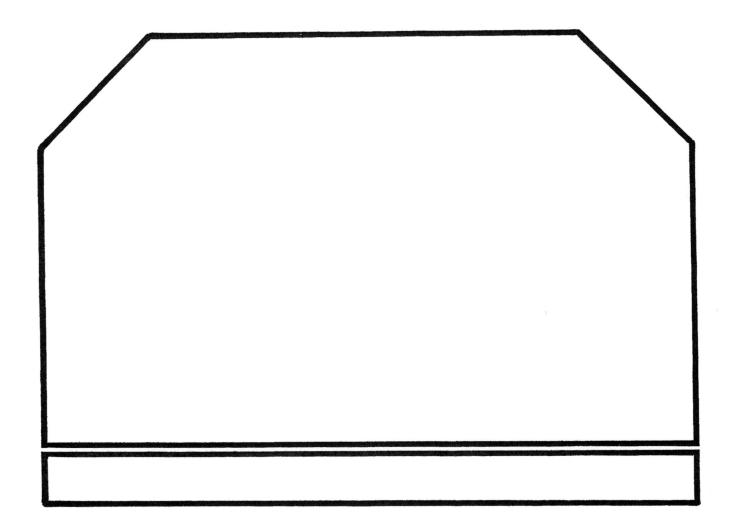

Japanese Wind Sock

EARLY ELEMENTARY WITH HELP; OLDER ALONE / 20-30 MINUTES

MATERIALS: World map, white 11x17-inch (27.5x42.5-cm) paper, pencils, colored markers, black fine-tip felt pens, yarn or string, chenille wires, hole punch, transparent tape, glue, scissors, measuring stick, paper clips.

PREPARATION: Cut yarn or string into 15-inch (37.5-cm) lengths and 30-inch (75-cm) lengths—one of each length for each child. Fold paper in half lengthwise and draw a fish shape (sketch a). Photocopy or draw one for each child.

PROCEDURE: Show Japan on a map. **What missionaries do we know who work in Japan? Who can tell me what a wind sock does?** (Shows direction the wind is blowing.) **When the wind blows through a wind sock, what will it do?** (Fill with air and float horizontally.) **The Japanese often make wind socks in the shape of one of their favorite fishes—the carp. When we see our wind socks floating on the breeze, we'll remember to pray for our missionaries in Japan.**

TO MAKE THE WIND SOCK, FOLLOW THESE STEPS:

Step 1: Cut out fish shape from folded paper.

Step 2: Unfold paper and use pencil to sketch details on fish such as scales, eyes and fins. Color with markers and use black felt pen to outline details on fish.

Step 3: Turn fish over, colored side down, and fold mouth opening down 1 inch (.25 cm). Squeeze a line of glue along folded area (sketch b).

Step 4: Lay a chenille wire over the line of glue. Fold paper over wire and hold in place with paper clips until glue dries.

Step 5: Roll fish's mouth into a circle shape. Twist chenille wires together to secure. Tuck wire ends inside.

Step 6: Glue seams of fish together (hold with paper clips while drying). Fold a small piece of tape over each side of mouth to reinforce (sketch c). Punch hole through each piece of tape and tie ends of shorter length of yarn through holes to make a bridle. Tie one end of longer length of yarn to the midpoint of bridle (sketch c).

Tie wind sock to pole or porch railing for decoration. When wind blows, wind sock will fill up with air and float horizontally.

ENRICHMENT IDEAS: Children, instead of teacher, draw their own fish (or other animal shape) on folded paper. To make a longer-lasting wind sock, use white fabric instead of paper.

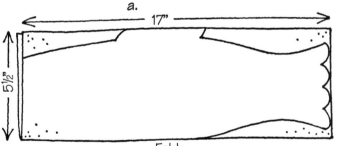

a.
17"
5½"
Fold

b.
Chenille wire
1"
Glue

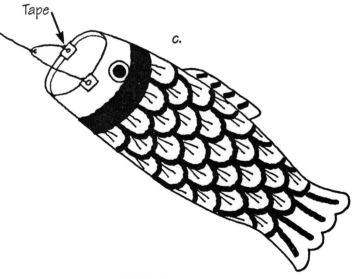

Tape
c.

Japanese Origami

YOUNGER ELEMENTARY / 15-20 MINUTES

MATERIALS: World map, origami (or-ih-GAH-mee) paper or other colored paper (gift wrap also works well), scissors, felt pens, measuring stick.

PREPARATION: If you do not have precut origami paper, cut paper into 7-inch (17.5-cm) squares.

PROCEDURE: Show a world map. **Where is the country of Japan located? What missionaries do we know who live in Japan? In Japan, many people like to fold paper to make the shapes of animals and other things. This kind of art is called origami (or-ih-GAH-mee). We're going to make origami dogs and cats.**

TO MAKE THE ORIGAMI ANIMALS, FOLLOW THESE STEPS:

For a dog:

Step 1: Fold paper in half (sketch a).

Step 2: Fold two narrow triangles, pointed ends down (sketch b). Crease folds.

Step 3: Draw eyes and nose (sketch c).

For a cat:

Step 1: Fold paper in half (sketch a).

Step 2: Fold the corners up for the ears—closer to the center than for the dog. Fold the top corner down (sketch d).

Step 3: Turn the paper over and draw the cat's face (sketch e).

ENRICHMENT IDEA: Bring an origami book (available at most libraries) and extra paper. Older children will enjoy making other animal shapes.

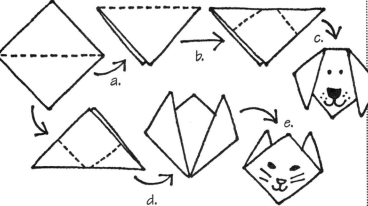

Mexican Cup Catch

EARLY ELEMENTARY WITH HELP; OLDER ALONE / 20 MINUTES

MATERIALS: World map, construction paper in a variety of colors, string, hole punch, markers, transparent tape, craft knife, scissors, measuring stick; for each child—one large orange juice can, one 3/4-inch (1.9-cm) wooden bead.

PREPARATION: Cut off 2¾ inches (6.9 cm) from top of each orange juice can and discard (sketch a). Cut construction paper into 2x9-inch (5x22.5-cm) rectangles—one for each child. Cut string into 12-inch (30-cm) lengths—one for each child. Wrap a piece of tape around one end of each string and tie a knot at other end.

PROCEDURE: Show a map of the world. Invite children to point out Mexico. Talk about missionaries who live there. **We are going to make a cup catch game. This game is played by children in Mexico.**

TO MAKE THE CUP CATCH GAME, FOLLOW THESE STEPS:

Step 1: Use markers to decorate paper.

Step 2: Wrap paper around can and tape in place.

Step 3: With teacher's help, punch hole near top edge of can.

Step 4: Thread bead onto string and slide next to knot. Then tie another knot just below bead to secure (sketch b).

Step 5: Tie opposite end of string through hole in cup (sketch c). Hold cup and try to toss the bead into the cup.

Mexican Piñata

EARLY ELEMENTARY WITH HELP; OLDER ALONE / 20-30 MINUTES

MATERIALS: World map, tissue paper in a variety of bright colors, yarn, hole punch, glue, scissors, tape, measuring stick. For each child—one large paper grocery bag.

PREPARATION: Cut tissue paper into 3-inch (7.5-cm) wide strips. (Older children may do this step alone.) Cut yarn into 6-foot (1.8-m) lengths—one for each child.

PROCEDURE: Show world map. **Who can tell me where Mexico is? What missionaries do we know who work in Mexico? What are some of the things they do?**

The first piñatas came from Italy. They were clay pots filled with goodies, then broken. Italians brought this custom to Spain and the Spanish brought the custom to Mexico. The Mexican people began making piñatas from papier-mâche and decorating them with colored tissue paper. We'll make our own piñatas.

TO MAKE THE PIÑATA, FOLLOW THESE STEPS:

Step 1: Fold down top edge of bag (sketch a).

Step 2: Fringe bottom edges of tissue paper strips with scissors (sketch b).

Step 3: Glue top edge of fringed strip around bag at bottom (sketch c).

Step 4: Glue fringed strips in overlapping fashion, to cover glued area of previous strips. Glue fringed strips onto bag until entire bag is covered (sketch d).

Step 5: Punch holes about 2 inches (5 cm) apart along top edge of bag. Place tape over end of a length of yarn. Thread through holes (sketch d). Pull ends of yarn to gather top of piñata.

We can take our piñatas home and fill them with wrapped candies and small toys.

To use piñata: Fill piñata with small candies and toys. Tie yarn to a tree branch. With friends, take turns wearing a blindfold and swinging at piñata with a stick or rolled-up newspaper. (Keep children out of the area where stick is being swung.) When bag breaks, everyone scrambles to pick up goodies.

Fold

a.

b.

3"

c.

d.

Mexican Yarn Art

ALL AGES / 20 MINUTES

MATERIALS: World map, yarn in a variety of colors, cardboard, glue, craft sticks, scissors, measuring stick.

PREPARATION: Cut cardboard into 9-inch (22.5-cm) squares—one for each child. Cut yarn into 2-foot (.6-m) lengths—at least three different colors for each child.

PROCEDURE: Show a map of the world. **Where is Mexico? Name our missionaries in Mexico.**

Today we're going to make shapes with yarn. The Huichol (WHEE-chole) people of Mexico are famous for their yarn pictures. They use designs of birds, fish, deer, and other animals. To make their pictures, they press yarn into beeswax that is warmed by the sun. But we'll use glue!

TO MAKE YARN ART, FOLLOW THESE STEPS:

Step 1: Squeeze out a line of glue to make a design on the cardboard. Or cover an area of the cardboard with glue.

Step 2: Starting with the end of a long length of yarn, press it onto glue to make outline. Use a craft stick to press into place.

Step 3: Continue to fill in shape with other colors of yarn, working from the outside in. Cut yarn as needed. Fill all blank spaces with yarn.

Use finished design at home as a coaster or hang as a picture.

SIMPLIFICATION IDEA: For younger children, cut Con-Tact® paper into 9-inch (22.5-cm) squares— and glue the non-sticky side directly on top of a cardboard square (see sketch). Child peels off backing and sticks yarn onto Con-Tact® paper.

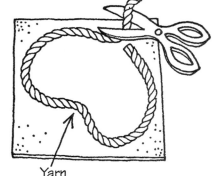

Yarn

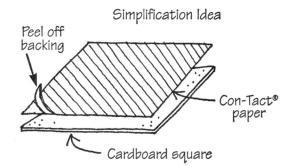

Simplification Idea

Peel off backing

Con-Tact® paper

Cardboard square

Native American Jackrabbits

EARLY ELEMENTARY WITH HELP; OLDER ALONE / 15-20 MINUTES

MATERIALS: World map, three corn husks and several feathers for each child, scissors, white glue, raffia (available at craft stores) or yarn, measuring stick.

PREPARATION: Cut yarn or raffia into 1-yard (1-m) lengths, one for each child. Soak dried corn husks in warm water for about 15 minutes to make them pliable or use green corn husks, if available.

PROCEDURE: Point to the southwestern United States on map. **What missionaries do we know who work with Native Americans? Many Native American tribes play a game like badminton. We'll make the game the way it is made by the Zuni** (ZOO-nee) **people of the Southwest. The "jackrabbit" is like a shuttlecock. It will be hit with an open hand instead of a racket. It's called a jackrabbit because when it flies, it sounds like a jackrabbit hopping over snow.**

TO MAKE THE JACKRABBIT,
FOLLOW THESE STEPS:

Step 1: Form a cross with two wide, flat corn husks. Roll a third corn husk into a small, flat square. Place this in center of the crossed husks (sketch a).

Step 2: Lift the two ends of the bottom husk and pinch them together at the center over the folded husk, then lift the other two ends in the same way (sketch b).

Step 3: While pinching the husks together, slip the feathers into the center of the pinched husks (sketch c).

Step 4: Wrap raffia or yarn around the pinched ends (sketch d), binding husk ends securely around the shafts of the feathers. Stop winding about ½ inch from the ends of the husks and knot the raffia, then tuck ends under and glue the area to secure.

Step 5: Fluff the feathers, pulling them out a bit to be well-balanced in the center.

To play, two or more players take turns batting the jackrabbit into the air with the palm of one hand. The one to hit it the most times without missing wins the round. Jackrabbits may also be hit between players standing in a circle.

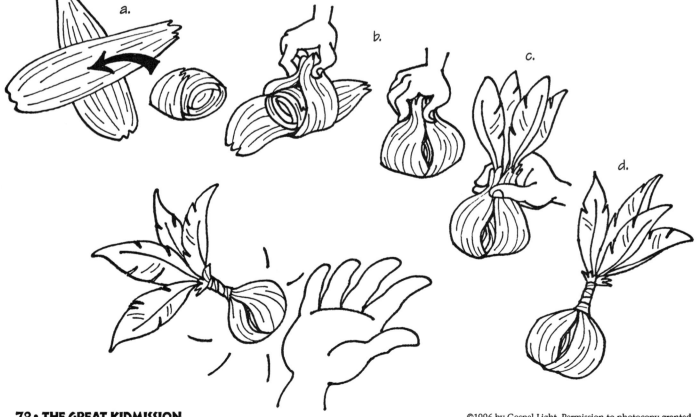

North African Headband

YOUNGER ELEMENTARY WITH HELP; OLDER ALONE / 30 MINUTES

MATERIALS: World map, pop-top tabs from soft drink cans (at least 15-20 for each child), chenille wires, scissors, measuring stick, hammer.

PREPARATION: Use a hammer on a hard, flat surface to flatten bent tabs and bend under any sharp edges. If younger children will be making this craft, precut chenille wires into 1-inch (2.5-cm) lengths.

PROCEDURE: Show a map of the world. **Who can show me where North Africa is? The area we call the Middle East? What missionaries do we know who work in these areas? Many of these people wear a piece of cloth over their heads to protect them from the sun and wind. They often wear a sort of chain made of silver coins and silver pieces over their headdresses. In North Africa, this chain is called a *zeriref*** (ZEHR-rih-ref). (Optional: Show pictures of zeriref from the *National Geographic* or another source.)

TO MAKE THE ZERIREF, FOLLOW THESE STEPS:

Step 1: If not already prepared, cut chenille wires into 1-inch (2.5-cm) lengths.

Step 2: Link 15-20 tabs together by twisting chenille wires between links (sketch a). Press twisted part of wire to back sides of the links. (Twisted wires can be pressed flat on a table as links are made.) Link tabs loosely enough that they can move.

Step 3: As headband is formed, check the fit around the child's head. It should fit around the head with two fingers' space to allow for wearing a cloth beneath it.

Step 4: Add tabs to bottoms of the links as desired. Leave them dangling free as decoration (sketch b).

Zeriref can be worn alone or over a piece of cloth draped over the head (sketch b).

SIMPLIFICATION IDEA: Use lightweight aluminum washers (available at hardware stores) in place of pop-top tabs.

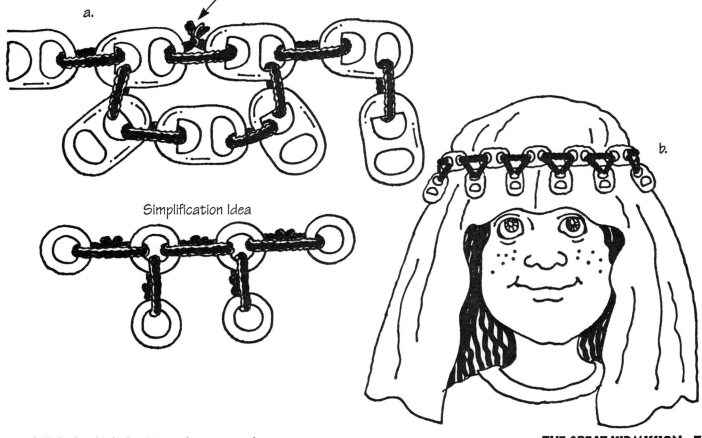

Bend twisted ends down and flatten

a.

Simplification Idea

b.

Russian Collage

ALL AGES / 20-30 MINUTES

MATERIALS: World map, 9x12-inch (22.5x30-cm) pieces of poster board for each child, fabric scraps, yarn, buttons, beads, pencils, scissors, glue.

PROCEDURE: Show map of the world. **Who can show me where Russia is located? Who do you know who came from Russia? What missionaries do you know there?** Volunteers respond.

In Russia, many children enjoy making very detailed collages, sometimes working on their collages over several days. They might use bits of corduroy to look like wood or might cut out tiny leaves from paper for the trees. Your collage may be a picture of anything you want.

TO MAKE THE COLLAGE, FOLLOW THESE STEPS:

Step 1: Choose a subject—either a picture of your room or your house, an outdoor scene or a still life. On posterboard, draw large and small shapes in drawing. Sketch this out lightly in pencil.

Step 2: Cut fabric into the shapes you have chosen and glue them onto the poster board.

Step 3: Think about how you could add small details using yarn, beads and buttons. Besides leaves on trees or tail feathers on a bird, it might be fun to make a window or door with a flap that can open to reveal a picture inside. Or, try using tiny pieces of fabric for bricks and stones. Even the sky could be a mosaic of many tiny pieces of different-colored fabric.

Russian Easter Eggs

ALL AGES / 20-30 MINUTES

MATERIALS: World map, white paper, scissors, crayons, black paint, pencils, paint brushes, small containers.

PREPARATION: Pour a small amount of paint into small containers, one for every two children.

PROCEDURE: On a world map, invite children to point to the CIS or Russia. **What missionaries do we know in Russia? in the other countries in that area? In Russia and other areas of Eastern Europe, many people decorate eggs at Easter time. They call these eggs** *pasanky* **(PEA-son-key). And they do more than dip the eggs in coloring. They paint very detailed designs on each egg. Each one is an egg-shaped work of art! We are going to decorate eggs like people do in Russia. But our eggs won't break.**

TO MAKE RUSSIAN EASTER EGGS, FOLLOW THESE STEPS:

Step 1: Cut out a large egg shape from a piece of paper.

Step 2: Draw a design in pencil on the egg shape.

Step 3: Fill in all the areas you want to color with crayons. Colored areas should be heavily covered with crayon if you do not want them covered by black paint.

Step 4: Paint over the whole egg shape with black paint. Let dry.

South American Loom Weavings

OLDER ELEMENTARY / 30-40 MINUTES

MATERIALS: World map, corrugated cardboard, yarn in a variety of colors, scissors, measuring stick.

PREPARATION: Cut cardboard into 5x6-inch (12.5x15-cm) rectangles. Cut slits about ½-inch (1.25 cm) deep and about ½-inch (1.25 cm) apart on both the short ends of the cardboard (sketch a). Cut most of the yarn into 3-foot (1-m) sections. Cut one 6-ft. (1.8-m) length for each child. (If you have enough time, let children cut slits.)

PROCEDURE: Display map. **Point to South America on our map. Where is Central America? Mexico? What missionaries do we know who work in these areas? In all of these countries, many people weave blankets, clothing, belts and bags. Today we're going to make our own weavings. They will remind us to pray for people who live in these countries.**

TO MAKE THE WEAVING, FOLLOW THESE STEPS:

Step 1: Using the 6-ft. (1.8-m) length of yarn, slip one end into the first slit on the bottom left side of the cardboard and through corresponding top slit. Continue winding yarn around cardboard to end on the bottom of the right side (sketch b). This is called the *woof.* Cut off any long ends.

Step 2: Tie end of first weaving length to woof. Weave yarn *under,* then *over* to the end of the first row. To weave next row, weave yarn *over* and *under* to the end.

Step 3: Repeat this weaving pattern for rows 1 and 2. Note: Do not pull yarn tightly across woof; it should be loose enough that woof yarns stay straight (sketch c). As each row is finished, use fingers to comb each row down snugly against the previous row. Tuck knots underneath when tying on new yarn.

Step 4: When weaving is about 1 inch (2.5 cm) from the top of loom, finish the row and tie end of weaving yarn to woof. Turn loom over and cut the strands that cross the loom through the middle (sketch d). Then tie every two loose ends together to make fringe. Trim fringe to desired length (sketch e).

SIMPLIFICATION IDEA: To make the weaving go more quickly, use rug yarn or other thick yarn.

COSTUME IDEA: Children may make a series of weavings and stitch them together to make belts.

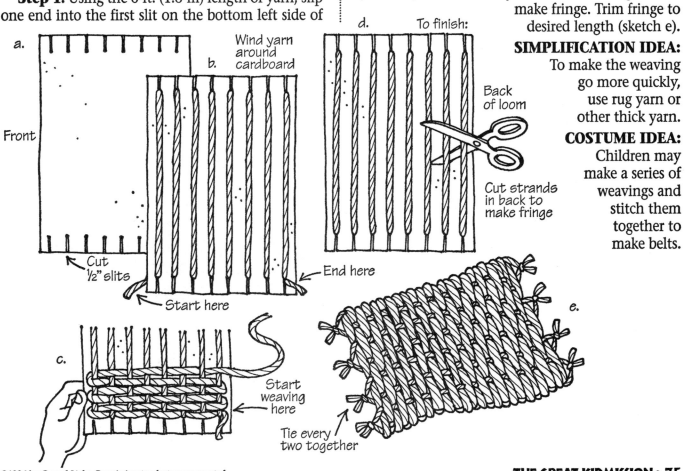

a. Front — Wind yarn around cardboard — Cut ½" slits — Start here — End here — b.

d. To finish: — Back of loom — Cut strands in back to make fringe

c. — Start weaving here — Tie every two together — e.

Swedish Heart Baskets

EARLY ELEMENTARY AND UP / 20 MINUTES, INCLUDING DRYING TIME

MATERIALS: World map, Swedish Heart Basket Pattern, colored paper, paste or glue stick, scissors.

PREPARATION: Photocopy the pattern onto colored paper, at least one for each child.

PROCEDURE: Show map of the world. **Where in the world is Sweden? What missionaries do we know who work there?** Volunteers tell. **Today we're going to make heart baskets, called** *julgranskorgar* (YOOL-gran-skor-gahr) **in Swedish. In Sweden, people make these for holidays and fill them with little candies.**

We can use our baskets to hold papers with prayer requests for our missionaries written on them. Or we can fill them with candies and nuts and give them to people.

TO MAKE A BASKET, FOLLOW THESE STEPS:

Step 1: Cut out the two circles. Fold both circles in half.

Step 2: Slide one folded half-circle inside the other so the folds meet in a point at the bottom (sketch a).

Step 3: Paste inner half to outer half.

Step 4: Cut a strip of paper and paste each end to each inner side of the basket for handle (sketch b).

Step 5: Let paste dry. Fill baskets.

ENRICHMENT IDEA: Children decorate outsides of baskets by attaching small stickers or drawing with glitter pens.

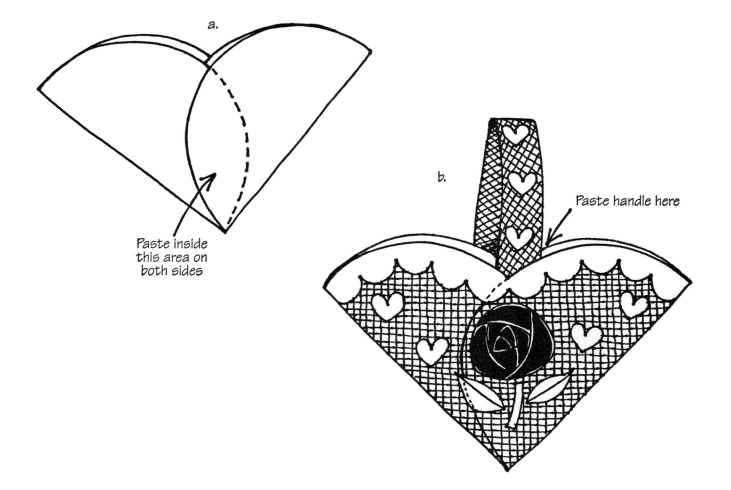

a.

Paste inside this area on both sides

b.

Paste handle here

Swedish Heart
Baskets Patterns

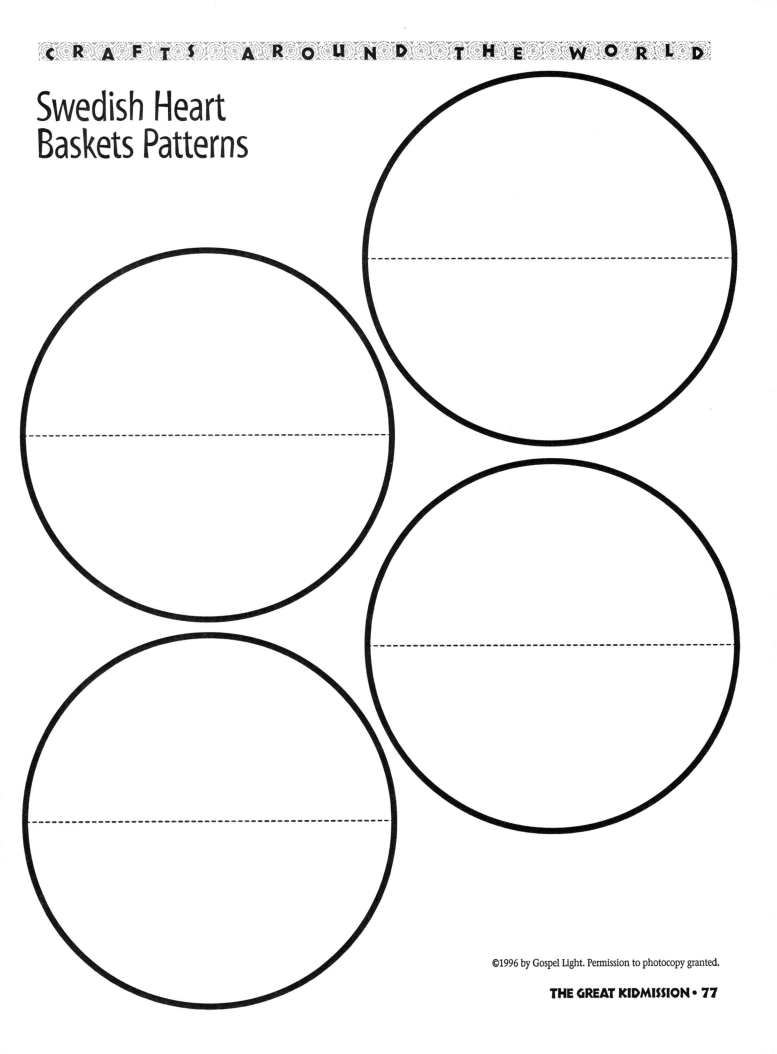

Swedish Snowflakes

ALL AGES / 15-20 MINUTES

MATERIALS: World map, white paper, several paper cups and plates, pencils, scissors.

PROCEDURE: Display a world map. **Where is Sweden? Do you know anyone whose family came from Sweden? What missionaries do you know who live in Sweden? It snows a lot in Sweden. To celebrate the beauty of the snow, Swedish children make paper snowflakes and put them in their windows. We can make snowflakes, too.**

TO MAKE A SNOWFLAKE, FOLLOW THESE STEPS:

Step 1: Trace a circle using a plate or cup onto paper. (Make larger circles for younger children.) Cut out the circle.

Step 2: Fold the circle in half once, then again, then two more times (sketches a-d). Snip shapes out of the sides (sketches e-f). Do not make too many cuts on the fold so the paper will stay as one piece when it is opened.

Make as many snowflakes as time allows.

Vietnamese Lanterns

YOUNGER ELEMENTARY / 15 MINUTES

MATERIALS: World map, 9x12-inch (22.5x30-cm) sheets of red construction paper, scissors, pencil, markers, stapler, measuring stick.

PREPARATION: Fold a piece of construction paper in half lengthwise for each child. Draw six straight lines, starting about ½ inch (1.25 cm) from the outer edge and ending at the fold. Lines should be 1 inch (2.5 cm) apart.

PROCEDURE: Show map of the world. **Who can show me where Vietnam is located? Who do you know who came from Vietnam? What missionaries do you know there? In Vietnam, people light lanterns during their Mid-Autumn Festival** (September).

TO MAKE A LANTERN, FOLLOW THESE STEPS:

Step 1: Unfold paper. On the blank side of prepared construction paper, draw pictures or designs with markers.

Step 2: Refold the paper with the designs on the inside, then cut on the lines, starting from the fold (sketch a).

Step 3: Refold paper so the design faces out, then roll it lengthwise. It will pop out in the middle, forming a tall lantern (sketch b).

Step 4: Overlap the edges of the paper and staple them together.

Step 5: Cut a strip of construction paper and staple it across the top of the lantern as a handle.

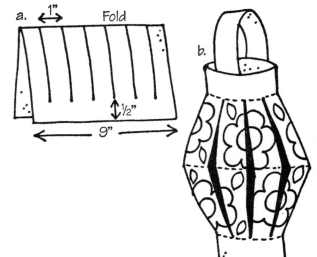

Anyone can tell the good news of Jesus!
Here are some projects the kids in your group can do to share the gospel
with the people around them and to help them better understand missions.

Good News Posters

ALL AGES / 15-20 MINUTES

MATERIALS: Bible, poster board or large sheets of paper, pencils, crayons, markers, scissors, glue.

PROCEDURE: Ask a volunteer to find and read Matthew 28:19,20 in a Bible. Ask, **How would you say this verse in your own words? Why is it important to tell others about Jesus?** After children answer say, **Today we'll make posters about the good news God wants us to share with others. Each of you may think of a short phrase that tells some good news about Jesus.** Give some examples: "Jesus is alive," "Jesus is God's Son" or "Jesus loves you."

TO MAKE A POSTER, FOLLOW THESE STEPS:

Step 1: After choosing the words for your poster, use crayons or markers to write the phrase in block letters on paper (see sketch).

Step 2: Cut out the letters.

Step 3: Glue them onto the poster board.

Step 4: Draw pictures around, above or below the words to illustrate the phrase. You may want to decorate the letters and the borders of the poster also.

Step 5: Help each other as you hang the posters; talk together about the meaning of each poster as you work.

Finished posters may hang in the Missions Center, on a classroom wall, in a hallway or church vestibule for a few days. Then invite children to take the posters home and hang them in their rooms as a way to tell the good news about Jesus to their friends.

ENRICHMENT IDEA: Provide photocopies of clip art items that might enhance posters. Color, cut out and glue items to posters.

Good News Wall Hanging

OLDER ELEMENTARY / 20-30 MINUTES

MATERIALS: Bible, fabric such as muslin or burlap, scissors, measuring stick, glue, pencils, markers, several different colors of felt and/or fabric, stapler, a wire clothes hanger for each child.

PREPARATION: Cut muslin or burlap into rectangles approximately 12x18 inches (30x45 cm).

PROCEDURE: What words would you use to describe someone who is a missionary? Volunteers answer. **Listen to this verse to discover what Jesus said a missionary does.** Read Mark 16:15 from Bible. **Jesus wants all of His followers to tell people the good news of God's love. We can do that at home, with our friends or anyplace. One way we can be witnesses to God's love is to make wall hangings for our homes that tell about God's love.** Show the materials you have collected. **What are some symbols, words or pictures that will tell about God's love and what He sent Jesus to do for us?** (Symbols such as a heart, cross, Bible; words such as "God loves you," "Jesus is my best Friend,"

"God's love lasts forever"; pictures such as two hands clasped, happy faces, Jesus with a child.) **What could you tell the person about your wall hanging that will help him or her know more about God's love?**

TO MAKE THE WALL HANGING, FOLLOW THESE STEPS:

Step 1: Choose a symbol, word or picture.

Step 2: Lightly outline design on the muslin (or burlap) with pencil.

Step 3: Cut the pieces for the design from the fabric and/or felt scraps.

Step 4: Glue the pieces onto the muslin (or burlap) and let dry.

Step 5: Decorate your wall hanging by drawing on it with markers.

Step 6: Fold the top edge over a wire hanger and staple (see sketch). Display wall hangings in your classroom until you take them home.

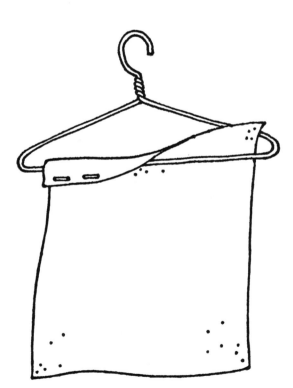

Missions Then and Now

ALL AGES / 15-20 MINUTES

MATERIALS: Bibles, 12x18-inch (30x45-cm) sheets of construction paper, 8½x11-inch (21.25x27.5-cm) sheets of white paper, pencils, crayons or markers, glue, information from your church about missionaries your church supports (locations, occupations of missionaries, etc.).

PREPARATION: Gather and organize information about missionaries your church supports. (If you have used the KidMission Reports, add them to your information.)

PROCEDURE: Missionaries leave their own homes to go to places where people need to learn of God's love. Ask an older child to read Acts 22:15. **Today we're going to work together to make a display showing missionaries in New Testament times and missionaries today. We'll call our display "Missions Then and Now."**

We're each going to find a buddy (pair an older with a younger child, for help with reading). **Then I'm going to give each team a Bible verse that tells about something missionaries did in Bible times. Your job is to find out how missionaries do those same**

things today. Assign each pair a Bible reference to read about some things missionaries did in New Testament times: Acts 16:11 (traveled by boat); Acts 17:2 (spoke in synagogues); Acts 19:1 and 20:13 (walked and/or sailed from town to town); 1 Corinthians 1:1,2 (wrote letters). Place the missionary information where all children can use it.

TO MAKE THE DISPLAY, FOLLOW THESE STEPS:

Step 1: With your buddy, find and read the Bible verse. Talk about what this verse tells you about a missionary.

Step 2: Look through the missionary information. Compare the actions of missionaries in New Testament times with the actions of missionaries today. **How do you think missionaries do the things you read about in the Bible today? What is different? What is the same?**

Step 3: Work with your buddy to draw pictures or write sentences on white paper to answer the questions in Step 2.

Step 4: Glue the white paper to folded construction paper sheets to make a display as shown in sketch.

Invitation to Church

ALL AGES / 15-20 MINUTES

MATERIALS: Construction paper in bright colors, scissors, glue, pencils, white paper, fine-tip felt pens.

PREPARATION: If you will be using this invitation for a specific event, consider photocopying an announcement with time, place and date included for children to cut out and glue to inside of invitation.

PROCEDURE: Invite children to name friends in their neighborhoods who don't go to church. **Many grown-ups will let their children come to church with you if you ask. You can ask your mom or dad to ask a friend's parents if their children can attend church with you. If we are having a special program at church, we can invite our friends to come. Or if we're going to have a fun activity here at church, we can invite them to do it with us. Today we're going to make invitations to** (church, special event, activity). **We'll give them to friends in our neighborhoods. We can also pray for opportunities to invite neighbors or school friends to church with us. Tell your friends about times when you have fun here at church.**

TO MAKE THE INVITATION, FOLLOW THESE STEPS:

Step 1: Fold construction paper into a card shape.

Step 2: Decorate it any way you like on the outside (sketch a).

Step 3: On the inside of the invitation, write (or have someone else write) the words you want on your invitation. Include the name of your friend(s) and be sure to sign the invitation.

Step 4: Glue the announcement (if provided) onto the other half of the inside page (sketch b). Or write the time, place, date and name of event on white paper and glue it to the other half of the inside page.

a.　b.

Missionary Prayer Calendar

OLDER ELEMENTARY / 15-20 MINUTES

MATERIALS: Calendar Grid Pattern, pens or pencils, fine-tip felt pens, 9x12-inch (22.5x30-cm) construction paper, glue.

PREPARATION: Photocopy one pattern for each child. Assemble as much missionary literature as you can about specific families or individuals (KidMission Reports, prayer cards, brochures, etc.).

PROCEDURE: Missionaries really need our prayers. They are doing exciting work, but it is hard work, too. It is important for us to ask God to help them in many ways. He hears our prayers and He will answer. One easy way to remember to pray each day for a missionary is to pray for a different need that a missionary (family) has.

If children have not done so before, invite them now to look at the missionary information about missionaries your church supports.

TO MAKE THE PRAYER CALENDAR, FOLLOW THESE STEPS:

Step 1: Choose a missionary to "adopt" for prayer purposes.

Step 2: Glue the Calendar Grid to a sheet of construction paper.

Step 3: Using the information about your missionary (and family), fill in a prayer request for each day of the week. If you run out of ideas from the information you have, use some of these:

◆ Help in knowing God better themselves, through reading the Bible and prayer.

◆ For physical strength, for the family to understand each other, to have desire to help each other.

◆ For the people that work together in the mission: to understand each other, love each other and for wisdom to solve problems that come up in the way God wants them to.

◆ Help with speaking or writing the language, help with loneliness or missing home.

◆ For God's help in telling others about Jesus, in teaching others about God's Word.

MISSIONARY PRAYER CALENDAR

Monday	Tuesday	Wednesday	Thursday
Friday	Saturday	Sunday	

Here is a selection of service projects that can be used in a variety of ways with kids of all ages or can serve as an inspiration for service projects that are unique to your group!

Adopt a Missionary Kid

ALL AGES / 15-20 MINUTE START-UP TIME

MATERIALS: KidMission Report or other missionary family information, poster board and markers, communication materials (paper and pencils, audio cassettes, video cassettes, etc.).

PREPARATION: Use the completed KidMission Report Form (p. 10) for the names, ages and interests of children of the missionaries your church supports.

PROCEDURE: Using the information you have gathered, make an "Adopt a Missionary Kid" Poster for your classroom. Post a KidMission Report on each poster or list names, ages and interests of each child. If you have photographs, add them to the poster.

Invite children in your church who are near these children's ages to "adopt" a missionary kid by becoming a pen pal. (More than one child can be the same missionary kid's pen pal.) This may be done not only by writing to the child, but also through exchanging audio cassettes, video cassettes, faxes or E-mail with him or her.

Provide a sign-up sheet for those adopting a missionary kid; from time to time, ask that child to report on prayer requests and answers and other news he or she has received from the missionary kid.

This can be elaborate, including gifts and cards for birthdays and holidays, or it can be as simple as sending E-mail messages. Adjust the level of complexity according to the ages of children in your group, the needs of the missionary kids, and the amount of money available for the project.

Woven Straw Wreath

OLDER ELEMENTARY / 15-20 MINUTE START-UP TIME

MATERIALS: World map, raffia in a variety of colors, masking tape, measuring stick, contact cement, scissors, fishing line.

PREPARATION: Cut raffia into 3-foot (.9-m) lengths—three for each child. Cut fishing line into 6-inch (15-cm) lengths—one for each child.

PROCEDURE: Show world map and talk about missionaries or projects that need support. **Straw decorations are popular in countries all over the world. Today we will be making straw wreaths** (to sell to earn money for our missions project, to remind us to pray for a missionary).

TO MAKE THE STRAW WREATH, FOLLOW THESE STEPS:

Step 1: Tie ends of three lengths of raffia paper together in a knot, leaving a 1-inch (2.5-cm) tail above knot (sketch a).

Step 2: Tape tail of knot onto a hard surface. Braid strips loosely together until approximately 4 inches (10 cm) are left (sketch b). Remove tape from braid.

Step 3: Hold both ends of braid together to form a heart shape. Wrap one loose strand several times around the other five strands (sketch c). Use contact cement to glue in place. Hold until dry.

Step 4: Trim ends to leave a small fringe. Tie ends of fishing line to high points on either side of heart (sketch d). The fishing line will help wreath retain its shape and provide a hanger.

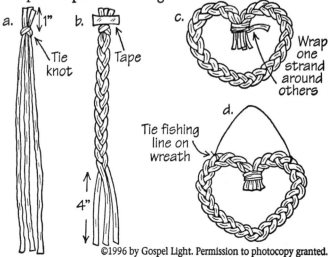

a. ↕1" Tie knot b. Tape c. Wrap one strand around others

4"

d. Tie fishing line on wreath

Missionary Care Package

ALL AGES / 15-30 MINUTE START-UP TIME; ONE OR MORE DAYS, DEPENDING ON OPTION

MATERIALS: Bibles, completed KidMission Report Form, materials for projects you choose to complete (see options below).

PREPARATION: If possible, use the KidMission Report Form (p. 00) information, names and birth dates of missionary family members. Optional—obtain a photograph of the family.

PROCEDURE: Ask a volunteer to locate and read Mark 16:15 in Bible. **What does Jesus tell us to do in this verse?** Volunteer answers. **Missionaries obey this verse by telling other people about God's great love and that He sent Jesus, His Son, to be our Savior and friend. Often, missionaries do this in countries that are far away. If you lived in a country far away from your home and friends, how do you think you might feel?** Volunteers respond. **While missionaries love the job they do, they always enjoy receiving packages from home. They might miss a particular treat they enjoyed at home such as M&M's or Starburst. Today we are going to work together to make a care package for the** (insert name) **missionary family.** Tell children about the family you have chosen. Then lead children to complete one or more of the following options:

***Option 1:* Birthday Cards:** Children use construction paper, stickers and markers to make birthday cards for each person in the missionary family. Enclose each person's birthday cards in envelopes labeled "Do not open until (date of person's birthday)." Or mail them prior to each person's birthday, allowing ample time for foreign mail service.

***Option 2:* Cassette Messages:** Children record messages on tape recorder. Each message should tell something about the child who is sending the message: child's family, his or her favorite activities, etc. Children may also sing a song, tell a joke, etc. Encourage children to ask the missionaries to send them a cassette in return.

***Option 3:* Comic Strip Collections:** Provide comic strip pages from newspapers. Include as many colored pages as possible. Children cut out their favorite comic strips and glue them onto sheets of paper. Punch holes in left margin of each sheet and tie together with yarn to make a book.

***Option 4:* Small Gifts:** Children bring stickers, favorite treats (Starburst, M&M's), pencils, crayons, markers, rubber stamps and stamp pad.

Collect completed projects(s) and mail to the missionary family.

Bread Dough Napkin Rings

FUND RAISER/OLDER ELEMENTARY / TWO-DAY PROJECT

MATERIALS: Heart and Dove Napkin Ring Patterns, lightweight cardboard, pencil, scissors, rolling pin, oven, dull kitchen knife, acrylic paint or sealer, brush; for dough—1 large bowl, 1 small bowl, flour sifter, wooden spoon, 2 cups flour (NOT self-rising), 1 cup cornstarch, 1 cup salt, 1 tsp. glycerin, 1 cup water (this recipe makes enough dough for eight to twelve napkin rings).

PREPARATION: Photocopy a set of patterns for every two or three students.

PROCEDURE: What does a heart usually make you think of? a dove? What are some ways God has shown love for us? What are ways we can show God's love to people who are far away? to missionaries?

We're going to make napkin rings that we are going to sell. We'll use the money we make to (support an orphan in another country, help a missionary, etc.).

TO MAKE THE NAPKIN RINGS, FOLLOW THESE STEPS:

Step 1: Glue napkin ring patterns to cardboard and cut them out.

Step 2: Make dough. Sift flour, cornstarch and salt into large bowl. In small bowl, mix glycerin and water, stirring well. Slowly add wet mixture to dry ingredients, stirring constantly. Knead dough until stiff and smooth—about five minutes.

Step 3: Roll out dough ¼-inch thick with rolling pin.

Step 4: Lay napkin ring patterns on top of rolled dough. Cut out napkin rings by cutting around patterns. Use tip of pencil to make designs in the dough. Repeat until all dough is used.

Step 5: Place napkin rings on cookie sheet and bake in oven at 275°F (35°C) for one hour. Turn oven off and allow napkin rings to cool in oven for one hour to eliminate cracking.

Step 6: Paint napkin rings with acrylic paint and/or spray with sealer.

One way to sell these napkin rings is to display them on a table after a service with a poster giving the price and the purpose of the fund-raising. Students remain at the table to collect the money for the napkin rings and explain their missions project.

GAMES

Games are more than just a way to "do something fun." Children have a genuine need for movement. And they certainly need to move more often than adults do! Head off the restlessness that comes with sitting still too long by planning for frequent changes of pace. By playing games in the middle of your program time, you give children a chance to move, to "let off steam" and to prepare themselves mentally and physically for a quieter activity.

Because all children love and need play, **Games Around the World** provide children some play experiences that connect them to the lives of children in another country. Both their bodies and their imaginations will be involved!

When you see children are beginning to get restless, but it's not yet game time, use one of the **Fun Fillers** to give them a quick, fun-time activity that won't throw you off schedule. When children get enough activity time, they are usually more cooperative and helpful when it's time for a quiet activity.

As a wise woman once said: "God put the wiggles in children; don't you try to take them out!"

Here is a collection of games to enhance children's awareness of the world around them and show them the ways children play in other countries.

Big, Big World

ALL AGES / ACTIVE GAME

MATERIALS: Chalk, world map of the seven continents (see Map of the World Patterns 1 and 2, pp. 00-00).

PREPARATION: Using world map as a guide, draw the seven continents in chalk on a playground surface (asphalt or concrete), each continent large enough for a group of children to stand inside.

PROCEDURE: Assemble children at edge of chalked world map. Ask volunteers to name a continent until all seven are named. Each time one is named say, **People wearing (blue), stand on (Asia).** Children move to stand on continent outlines. **There are missionaries all over the world.** Talk about specific missionaries. Show where they live on a world map. **What continent do you think (Mexico) is on?** Children guess which continent missionary's country is on by going to stand on that continent. Talk about some of the characteristics of the area where each missionary lives. **What do you think it's like in (Mexico)? Is it hot there? cold? Is it like a desert? a jungle?**

Crab Race

(Japanese Game)

ALL AGES / ACTIVE GAME

MATERIALS: None.

PLAY: To play this game, follow these steps:

Step 1: Form two relay teams of equal numbers of players.

Step 2: Set up a goal line for each team.

Step 3: The first player on each team leans backward and moves on all fours to look like a crab. The player must move in this position to the goal line and back.

Step 4: The player touches the next player who continues in the same way until all players have gone to the goal line and back. First team to finish wins.

Egyptian Stick Race

ALL AGES / ACTIVE GAME

MATERIALS: One 4-foot (1.2-m) stick for each player. (Broom handles work well.)

PLAY: To play this game, play a practice round first, following these steps:

Step 1: Players stand in a large circle, each person about 8 feet (2.4 m) from the next person, facing the middle of the circle. Each player holds a stick upright in the left hand, with one end of the stick on the ground.

Step 2: At a signal, each player simply opens his or her hand and lets go of his or her own stick, then races to catch the stick of the player to the right before that stick falls and touches the ground.

Step 3: If the stick falls and touches the ground, the player who did not catch it is out, along with the stick.

Step 4: Circle shrinks in size as more and more players are out. Last player remaining is the winner.

Forceball

(British or Australian Ball Game)

OLDER ELEMENTARY

MATERIALS: One basketball or kick ball, chalk or masking tape, measuring stick.

PREPARATION: Use chalk or tape to make two parallel lines about 3 yards (2.7 m) apart.

PLAY: Divide group into two teams. Players line up side by side with legs apart and feet touching as shown in sketch. Teams face each other. The object of the game is to roll the ball between the legs of the players on the opposing team. Players bat the ball to the opposite team using only their hands. Players cannot move their feet. Teams get one point every time the ball rolls through the opposing team's legs. Team with the most points wins.

Gorelki
(Russian Line Tag)

ALL AGES / ACTIVE GAME

MATERIALS: Rope or masking tape.

PREPARATION: Lay a 5-ft. (1.5-m) line of rope or masking tape in an open area.

PLAY: Choose one player to be "It." Rest of group lines up in two equal lines, about 10 feet (3 m) from the line. "It" stands behind the line. When "It" says, "Last ones run," the last ones run up the outside of their lines and join hands at the front of the lines before "It" can tag either one of them. If "It" tags a player before the pair can join hands, tagged player becomes "It" and they switch places.

Jan Ken Po
(Rock, Paper, Scissors in Japanese)

ALL AGES

MATERIALS: None.

PLAY: To play this game follow these steps: Demonstrate the three hand signs for rock, paper and scissors (see sketches). Then demonstrate the Japanese way to play this familiar game. Together say "Jan ken po" as each child shakes his or her fist up and down three times. On "po," make one of the three signs.

Here are the rules for the game:

If both people make the same sign, it is a tie.

Scissors wins over paper because scissors can cut paper.

Paper wins over rock because paper can cover rock.

Rock wins over scissors because rock can break scissors.

One point may be scored for each win. Partners may play until one person gets 10 points, then switch partners.

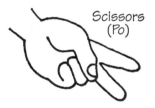

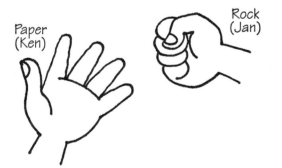

Jungle Sounds

ALL AGES

MATERIALS: None.

PLAY: Choose one child to be "It" and another to be the hunter. Other children choose an animal sound that all will imitate. "It" stands with his or her face to a wall (or blindfolded). Children move around so "It" will not know where children are. The hunter points to one child. Child makes the sound of the animal chosen by the group. "It" has to identify the animal and also the name of the child who made the sound. If "It" guesses both correctly, he or she changes places with the hunter. If not, "It" changes places with the child who made the animal sound.

Lame Chicken
(Chinese Relay Game)

ALL AGES (2 OPTIONS) / ACTIVE GAME

MATERIALS: Twenty sticks about 2 feet (.6 m) long, chalk or tape.

PREPARATION: Place 10 sticks on the ground, parallel to each other and about 1 foot (.3 m) apart (see sketch). Use chalk or tape to make a starting line about 15 feet (4.5 m) from the first stick. Make an identical course with the other 10 sticks.

PLAY: Divide group into two even teams. Teams stand in single file lines behind starting lines. At signal, first player on each team hops up to the first stick and hops over each stick to pick up the last one. Player then hops back over each stick, carrying stick that was picked up, and places stick about 1 foot (.3 m) in front of first stick. Player then hops back to tag next player in line. The next player repeats the process. First team to have all players complete the course wins.

Note: Players may hop on one foot or two, depending on the age and ability of the group.

Presohan

(Filipino Tag)

OLDER ELEMENTARY / ACTIVE GAME

MATERIALS: Chalk or masking tape, marker, measuring stick, empty soft drink can for each player.

PREPARATION: Use chalk or tape to mark a small *X* on the ground. Mark a "safety line" about 8 feet (2.4 m) from the *X* as shown in sketch.

PLAY: Give each player a soda can. Each player marks a can by writing his or her name on masking tape with marker, then placing masking tape on can. Choose one player to be the Prisoner. Prisoner sets his or her can on the *X* and stands behind it.

Players stand behind the "safety line" and take turns throwing their cans at the Prisoner's can. Once a player hits the Prisoner's can, the hitter must try to retrieve own can without being tagged by the Prisoner. (Prisoner may not tag hitter until Prisoner has returned own can to the *X*.) Hitter is safe when he or she crosses safety line. If the hitter is tagged, he or she becomes the new Prisoner. If a player throws but does not hit the Prisoner's can, he or she must wait until another player has hit the can. Then all players who have missed the can may run and try to retrieve their cans without being tagged by the Prisoner.

Tlachtli

(Mexican Ball Game)

OLDER ELEMENTARY / ACTIVE GAME

MATERIALS: Rubber playground ball, chalk or rope, markers to distinguish one team from another (handkerchief or cloth strip tied to arm), measuring stick, coin.

PREPARATION: Use chalk or rope to mark a 15x40-yard (40.5x108-m) rectangular playing area. Mark lines to divide the playing rectangle into four equal sections—two end courts and two middle courts (see sketch).

PLAY: Divide group into two even teams of 5-10 players each. Distribute markers to one team. Choose one player from each team to be the team captain. Have team captains call a coin flip to see which team is first. Teams take sides, facing each other. Each player is assigned to play in either the end court or middle court.

Play begins when teacher tosses ball into the air at center line. Each team tries to bump the ball to the other team's end line. The ball can only be hit with the hips, shoulders, knees or back—no hands, feet or heads. If the ball hits the ground, teacher tosses it up in the air from the point where it hit the ground. When a team scores a goal, the team gets 5 points and play starts over in the center. First team to score 25 points wins.

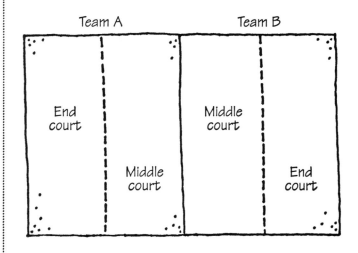

These quick and easy games are a good way to fill up shorter game times
or spots in the schedule where children need an activity break.

Balloon Burst

ALL AGES / ACTIVE GAME

MATERIALS: Balloons, slips of paper, pencil.

PREPARATION: On each slip of paper write an action for children to do (skip, walk backward, jump on right foot, do jumping jacks, etc.). Place one slip in each balloon. Inflate and tie balloon.

PLAY: Toss balloons into the air. Players each try to catch one, while trying to keep each other from catching the balloons by hitting them back up into the air.

After all balloons have been caught, children step on balloons to burst them. Then children follow the directions on the slip of paper. (For a nonreader, invite child to find a partner who can read the words and do the action together with him or her.)

Bible Memory Verse Version: Write a word or two of the Bible Memory Verse on each slip of paper instead of an action. Children play as above, then each bursts his or her balloon and reads the words on the paper. Children line themselves up in verse word order, by saying the words on his or her slip of paper. Then group repeats verse together several times.

Balloon Stomp

ALL AGES / ACTIVE GAME

MATERIALS: Balloons, string.

PREPARATION: For each child, inflate a balloon and tie a string to it. (Older players may do this step themselves.)

PROCEDURE: Each child ties (or teacher ties) an inflated balloon to his or her right ankle. At a signal, each child tries to burst the other children's balloons with his or her left foot. For younger children: If a child's balloon is burst, he or she may tie on another balloon and continue playing game. For older children: Player whose balloon is burst is out of the game.

Move as One

ALL AGES / ACTIVE GAME

MATERIALS: None.

PLAY: Divide class into groups of four to five children. Group members stand side by side in a straight line with their shoulders touching. Give the following directions: **left foot—step, right foot—step, left foot—stomp, right foot—stomp, slide to the left once, slide to the right once, left foot—stomp, right foot—stomp.** Groups perform the movements at the same time and in the same way. Repeat the pattern four times. Then have each group perform the pattern four times. Then have each group perform for the others. Optional—play music on cassette as groups do activity. This is not a "win or lose" type game, but a cooperative game.

Musical Chairs

ALL AGES / ACTIVE GAME

MATERIALS: One chair for each child, cassette recorder and music cassette or CD player and audio disc.

PREPARATION: Place chairs facing outward in a circle.

PLAY: Each child stands by a chair on outer edge of circle. Remove one chair from circle. As you play the music, children march around chairs. When you stop the music, each child tries to sit on a chair. Child without a chair signals the start of the next round. (Child may become "sound engineer" for the next round.)

CHALLENGE: During each round, older children must move in a certain way—hopping on one foot, taking baby steps, etc. to move around the circle.

Pass It!

ALL AGES

MATERIALS: Marble or penny for each group.

PLAY: Children sit in circles of no more than fifteen. One person is chosen to be "It." "It" stands in the middle of the circle and closes his or her eyes. Give one player in the circle a marble or penny. Players begin passing the marble or penny. At the leader's signal, "It" opens his or her eyes. All players pretend to be passing the marble or penny. "It" tries to guess who has the object by calling out that person's name or tapping the person on the shoulder. When "It" guesses correctly, he or she trades places with the person holding the marble or penny. If "It" has not guessed correctly after three tries, leader chooses someone else to be "It."

Shoe Scramble

ALL AGES / ACTIVE GAME

MATERIALS: Blindfold for each player.

PLAY: Players sit in circles of 4-10 members each and take off their shoes, then toss them into a pile in the middle of the circle. Blindfold each player, then mix up the shoes. On the word "go," players scramble to the shoe pile and try to determine which shoes are theirs by trying on different shoes. When players think they've found their own shoes, they put on both shoes. Play continues until everyone is wearing a pair of shoes. Remove blindfolds to see who is wearing whose shoes!

Split Up

ALL AGES / ACTIVE GAME

MATERIALS: None.

PLAY: All players walk or march around the room in a circle. The leader stands in the center of moving circle. When the leader calls out a number (from two to five), players divide into groups of the number called. For example, if the number two is called, players march in groups of two. Children continue walking or marching in these groups until the leader calls a new number.

Each leader has three turns and then chooses someone to take his or her place. Players who cannot fit into a group stand by leader until they form their own group or until next number is called.

ENRICHMENT IDEA: To make the game more challenging, caller in the center gives a number and a way to move (tiptoe, giant steps, crab walk, etc.).

DRAMA

Because children learn best when all of their senses are fully involved in an activity, drama becomes a natural learning tool! Whether recording sound effects, "hamming it up" as a talk-show host or reading the lines of a simple skit, drama activities involve a child in sight and sound, motion and touch, and most of all, imagination!

Consider using some of these activities even if you aren't the "dramatic type." Or invite another adult who enjoys kids to become the head of the "drama department." You'll find that children's level of enthusiasm and creativity will make the extra effort well worthwhile!

Drama activities can be a delightful accent to any missions program.

Involve children in reviewing a Bible story or expanding their missions horizons.
The following activities are easily done with materials on hand for immediate dramatic excitement!

Bible Story Puppets

ALL AGES / 15-20 MINUTES

MATERIALS: Bible, large sheets of white construction paper, stapler, transparent tape, pencils, scissors, markers, newspapers, paper plates cut in half.

PREPARATION: Make a sample puppet following directions below.

PROCEDURE: After the Bible story, invite children to retell story action. **(Lydia) shared the good news of Jesus. We can tell the good news about Jesus to our friends and family just as (Lydia) did.** Show your completed puppet. **Let's make Bible story puppets. We need to make puppets for** (Paul, Luke and Silas, several women and Lydia). Each child decides which puppet to make. (Several children may make a puppet of the same character.)

Children make puppets following these directions: Tape or lay two sheets of white construction paper on top of each other. One child lays down with his or her head and shoulders on paper while a partner traces around the first child. Partners trade places and repeat procedure with two more sheets of paper. Children cut out head outlines, then staple the two outlines together, leaving an opening at the bottom (sketch a).

Use markers to draw faces on puppets, then crumple the newspaper sheets and carefully stuff puppet heads. Staple the openings closed. Tape or staple a paper plate half on back of each puppet head for a handle (sketches b, c).

When children have completed their puppets, they may use them to act out the events in the Bible story in small groups or all together.

For younger children, read the Bible story aloud slowly again, pausing to let characters do the actions.

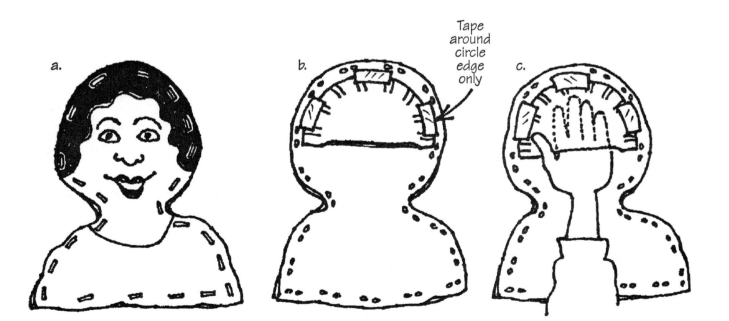

a.

b.

Tape around circle edge only

c.

Missions Talk Show

ALL AGES / 15-20 MINUTES

MATERIALS: Real or pretend microphone, chairs.

PREPARATION: Make arrangements with one of the following people to come and talk with children about missions: a retired missionary, a missionary home on furlough or a representative of a local missions organization. Set up a "talk show set" at the front of the room.

PROCEDURE: Before the visitor arrives, invite the children to think of questions for the guest. Write these down. Include some open-ended, "what-do-you-think?" kinds of questions to promote discussion.

Here are some sample questions to get you started.

What country do you live and work in? Where is it?

What are ways you tell people about Jesus?

What is your church like?

What kinds of problems do missionaries you know face?

What is the (scariest, most exciting) thing that has happened to you or a missionary you know?

What can missionaries do when it is dangerous to tell others about Jesus?

What is the best thing that has happened to you or a missionary you know?

What do you think missionaries need most?

Using the prop microphone, play the role of talk show host. **Good evening. I'm** (your name or a "stage name") **and this is— MissionTalk! Our guest tonight is** (name of missionary). Don't be afraid to "ham it up"! Ask the questions you have written down. Then take questions from the audience as you move through the group.

Sound-Effects Story Drama

ALL AGES / 15-20 MINUTES

MATERIALS: Bibles, cassette recorder and blank cassette, paper and pencils, props for sound effects.

PROCEDURE: After the Bible story, help the children recall the order of events. **Describe what happened in our Bible story. Where did the people go? How did they get there? What happened next?**

Today we are going to make a tape recording of some of the Bible verses that tell what happened in our Bible story. We'll add as many sound effects as we can. Read selected verses aloud from Bible story with children. Invite volunteers to tell in their own words what happened. Help children plan what they will record. **Some of you may read the Bible verses and others will make the sound effects.** Suggested sound effects: voices humming a familiar song, doors banging, bike chains rattling, sounds of people running, wind howling or whistling, water sounds. List children's ideas on paper. Children practice reading verses and making sound effects several times before recording. Play recording today during Response Time or make it part of a cassette you send to a missionary child.

SKITS AND HOW TO USE THEM

Skits are an involving and enjoyable way for young learners to grasp basic concepts about missions. Whether skits are read aloud, used with puppets or actually memorized and performed, dramatic involvement heightens children's interest and understanding. The audience not only always enjoys a skit—but also the players often learn valuable lessons by their involvement.

Performance of these skits need not be complicated: the use of any prop can be pantomimed in performance and the skit can always be used in a readers' theater setting. Consider pulling aside several early arrivals and giving them a skit to practice while they wait for the session to begin. Early arrivals are not left wandering and the skit is ready to be read or performed in short order!

The skits can be used as an opening "hook" at the beginning of Bible story time, as an opening drama for the day's program, as a learning activity or during Response Time, to reinforce a concept from the Bible story. A skit can also be a fun way to close the day's program, allowing time for several groups of children to take turns reading through the lines.

If time allows, use a skit in Sunday School or church the week before your missions conference begins to heighten interest in the upcoming conference.

For Readers' Theater

Divide into small groups (each group the size of the number of characters in the skit). Give each child a script and assign each one a part to read. Children in each small group simply read their parts at the appropriate time. If time allows, come together later in a large group. Invite volunteer readers to read the play in front of the rest of the group.

For Performance

Hand out scripts to children or youth group members several days in advance to learn lines for performance.

Depending on the interest level of your kids and the schedule you choose, kids could create backdrops, props, sound effects or costumes in addition to performing.

AN INTERNATIONAL INCIDENT

What can real kids do to help real missionaries?

CHARACTERS:
- ☐ Grandma
- ☐ Laurel
- ☐ Matthew
- ☐ Narrator

SUGGESTED PROPS:
- ☐ Stack of mail for Grandma including one letter that can be ripped apart
- ☐ Letter, obviously taped together

NOTE: Names and needs of missionaries your church supports may be substituted for words in parentheses.

(GRANDMA enters stage left, looking at a paper.)

Grandma: The mail just came!

(MATTHEW and LAUREL enter.)

Laurel: Oh, did I get any letters?

Grandma: *(Looks through mail.)* Well, let's see. Here's a bill, junk mail, bill, junk mail...wait! Here's a real, live letter! And it's addressed to all of us.

Matthew: *(Tries to look over GRANDMA's shoulder.)* Who's it from?

Grandma: Hmmm... *(Looks at letter.)*...oh, it's from our friends the (Porters)...all the way from (Japan)!

Laurel: That's exciting! We haven't heard from them for a LONG time.

Grandma *(laughing)*: Oh, Laurel, it hasn't been that long.

Laurel: Well, open it quick! Open it! What do they say?

Matthew: *(Takes letter from over GRANDMA's shoulder and begins to open it.)* Be PATIENT, Laurel.

Laurel: *(Reaches for letter.)* It's not every day we get a letter from missionaries in (Japan). Hurry up!

Matthew *(pulling letter away)*: I'm going to see it first! Be PATIENT!

(LAUREL and MATTHEW fight over the letter, pulling on it.)

(Sound of paper ripping from offstage.)

Grandma *(shaking her head)*: Now look what you've done. The letter is torn. Oh, children!

Matthew *(quietly)*: I'm sorry, Grandma...

Laurel: I'll get the tape. Maybe we can tape the letter back together. *(She exits.)*

Grandma: Well, all right. *(Shakes torn letter at LAUREL.)* But be quick! I want to see what the (Porters) have to say, too!

(Curtain closes.)

(Curtain opens. MATTHEW, LAUREL and GRANDMA are onstage, looking down at letter that has been obviously taped together.)

Grandma: There now, that should hold the letter together.

Matthew: C'mon, let's read it!

Laurel: Yeah, what do they say?

Grandma: *(Moves head as if reading.)* Well, let's see...they say they have a BIG need right now.

Laurel: What is it?

Grandma: They say that (their car needs to be fixed...and Johnny fell down and broke his leg).

Matthew: Oh, that's terrible!

Grandma: *(Looks at LAUREL, then MATTHEW.)* So, you two scrappers! What could we do to help?

Laurel: Well...we could (send some get well cards to Johnny). I could ask my friends at Sunday School to help me with that.

Grandma: Good idea. Anything else we could do?

Matthew: Well, I've got $2.38 saved in my bank. Maybe we could send some money to (help fix their car).

Laurel: Yeah, and maybe I could talk to my Sunday School teacher about (taking a special offering).

Grandma: That's a good idea, Laurel. See, kids? We can do something to help, even though we are far away! I know God wants us to help our missionary friends. *(All exit.)*

Narrator: Who are some missionaries we know? (Children name several missionary families your church supports. Mention any special needs of these missionaries.) There are many ways we can help our missionaries. Let's name some ways. (Volunteers respond.)

Close by asking several children or adults to pray for these missionaries and their specific needs.

GOTTA TELL!

What news is so exciting you've just got to tell it?

CHARACTERS:
☐ Laurel
☐ Mom
☐ Narrator

SUGGESTED PROPS:
☐ Grocery sack filled with groceries
☐ An empty shelf

(LAUREL paces at stage right. Sound of opening door.)

Mom *(enters, carrying grocery bag and calling)***:** I'm home! Hello, Laurel. Have you been home long?

Laurel: *(Runs to MOM and hugs her.)* Oh, Mom, I've been home for the LONGEST time! It feels like I've been here for HOURS. I'm glad someone's finally home! I've got to TELL somebody!

Mom: *(Puts groceries in cupboard.)* I'm sorry, Laurel. Grandpa wanted to stop at the nursery for seeds and we had to buy groceries, too. Then we got caught in a lot of traffic and...

Laurel *(interrupting)***:** I couldn't find ANYONE to tell! You were gone, Matthew was gone, I called Sammie and she wasn't home, and...

Mom *(interrupting)***:** Slow down! What do you have to tell? Why did you want to talk to someone? Did something bad happen to you today?

Laurel: No, Mom! Nothing BAD happened! In fact, I've got GOOD news!

Mom: Well then, tell me quick! What's the good news?

Laurel: Today I saw Mr. Lee, the principal, and he told me I've been chosen to be a library helper! I'll get to help with the younger kids and help put books away. Oh, Mom, I'm so EXCITED!

Mom: *(Gives LAUREL a hug.)* Well! that is good news, Laurel.

Laurel: It sure is! And it sure feels GOOD to finally SHARE my good news!
(They exit together, arms around each other, still talking.)

Narrator: Laurel had some good news! She was really excited to tell her good news to her mom. Tell me about some good news you've been excited to tell. What does the Bible call "good news"? That's news we can be excited to tell, too!

GUESS WHO'S COMING TO DINNER?

Are missionaries different from everybody else?

CHARACTERS:
☐ Matthew
☐ Lucas, Matthew's little brother
☐ Mom
☐ Laurel, Matthew's sister
☐ Narrator

SUGGESTED PROPS:
☐ Baby blanket for Lucas
☐ Baseball hat for Matthew

(MATTHEW and LAUREL enter walking, stage right.)

Matthew: Hey, Laurel, who did Mom say is coming to dinner tonight?

Laurel: The Nicholsons. You know, the ones who send the letters with the stamps you keep collecting!

Matthew: Oh, yeah. They're missionaries, aren't they?

Laurel: Well, of course they are! So what?

Matthew: Well...uh...well, do you think they'll eat our FOOD?

Laurel *(stops walking, disgusted)***:** Matthew, of COURSE they will! Missionaries eat the same kind of food as we do! Except maybe when they're out being missionaries; then they might eat some things that are different.

Matthew: *(Stops, begins to turn away from LAUREL.)* Well, whatever they eat, I wish they weren't coming!

Laurel: Matthew, how come? They've got a boy your age.

Matthew: *(Turns back to LAUREL.)* I don't know...I guess it's just that I don't know what to say to them! I mean, they're so DIFFERENT!

Laurel: Matthew! Get a grip! Missionaries aren't from outer space or something! They just live in another country, that's all. And they live there for a really good reason—because they want to tell people about Jesus. Anyway, if you really want to know what to talk to them about, go ask Mom.

Lucas *(entering)***:** Hi, Maffew!

Matthew: Oh, hi, Lucas. *(Pauses.)* Hey, guess what?

Lucas: What, Maffew? Did Mom make cookies?

Matthew: No, Lucas. It's a bigger surprise than that. We're going to have missionaries for dinner tonight!

Lucas *(slowly)*: Missionaries? *(Uncertainly.)* Well, they SOUND good. Are they better than cookies?

Matthew: *(Grabs LUCAS by the arm.)* Lucas!!! Missionaries aren't something to EAT! They're people! They live in other countries so they can tell the people there about God and Jesus.

Lucas *(disappointed, looking down)*: Aw shucks, Maffew. Then what are they good for? Can I PLAY with them?

Matthew: Sure you can play with them! They're people just like anybody else! They have kids—even a boy my age. *(To himself.)* Maybe he'll know a game from the country they live in.

Lucas: Good! I LIKE games. The missionary game sounds fun! *(Exits.)*

Matthew: *(Calls after LUCAS.)* Missionaries isn't the name of a game, EITHER, Lucas! *(Looks at LAUREL and sighs.)* Oh, well..

Mom *(entering)*: Oh, Matthew! Good. I've been looking for you. Did you know that the Nicholsons have a boy your age?

Matthew: I know, Mom. But what can I talk with him about?

Mom: Well, let's see. You could ask their boy—his name is Jon—what kinds of games the children play where he lives.

Matthew *(laughing)*: Games? I thought of that one already, Mom! Or maybe Lucas thought of it for me.

Mom: Well, since they live in another country, eat different food, and live in a different kind of house...you could ask him, "Hey! Tell me about your everyday life. When do you get up? What do you have for breakfast?" You know, things like that, Matt.

Laurel: Sure! See, Matthew? It won't be such a big deal!

Matthew: Yeah, I guess we could talk about all of that stuff. In fact, Mom, I think having missionaries for dinner will be a DELICIOUS experience!

Mom *(confused)*: What?...

Matthew: *(Laughs.)* It's a joke, Mom. Ask Lucas!

(All exit.)

I'M GONNA BE A MISSIONARY

What does a person need to become a missionary?

CHARACTERS:
- ☐ Matthew
- ☐ Sammie
- ☐ Grandpa

SUGGESTED PROPS:
- ☐ List, pencil for Sammie
- ☐ Book and letter for Grandpa

(SAMMIE is looking at and checking off a list.)

Sammie: Let's see now, what else do I need? Jungle helmet, machete...mosquito repellent.... Hmmmm...if I'm going to be a missionary, I'll need a lot of stuff!

(A knock is heard offstage.)

Sammie: Come on in, the door's open.

Matthew *(entering)***:** Hi, Sammie. What are you doing?

Sammie: Hi, Matthew. Well, I'm working on my missionary list. I've decided to be a missionary! So, I'm trying to figure out what I need to take along.

Matthew: You're going to be a missionary? Where are you going to go? What's on your list to take along?

Sammie: I don't know where I'm going, but I DO want to be a missionary. It sounds so exciting! *(Shows list to MATTHEW. Points.)* Here's my list so far: jungle helmet, machete, and mosquito repellent. What do you think, Matthew?

Matthew: Jungle helmet? Machete? Mosquito repellent? What do you need those for?

Sammie: I dunno. But from what I've heard, it sounds like every missionary should have those things. What else do you think I need?

Matthew: *(Shrugs shoulders.)* I'm not sure. Let's go ask Grandpa.

Sammie: OK. *(They exit together. Curtain closes.)*

(GRANDPA comes onstage with book in his hand. Letter is sticking out of book. From offstage, MATTHEW calls.)

Matthew: Grandpa, Grandpa, where are you?

Grandpa: I'm on the porch, Matthew.

(MATTHEW and SAMMIE enter.)

Grandpa: Hi, kids.

Matthew: Hi, Grandpa. What are ya doing?

Grandpa: Oh, just putting some new stamps in my stamp collection! I got a letter this morning from a missionary friend in South America. And there was a new stamp on the envelope.

Sammie: Wow! Did you say missionary? *(Begins to talk fast.)* I've come to the right place! See, I'd like to be a missionary! What does your friend do? Where does he live? What did he need to take with him?

Grandpa *(laughing)***:** Hold it, Sammie! One question at a time. *(Shows SAMMIE the letter.)* My friend lives in Lima, Peru. He's a doctor. His wife is a nurse.

Sammie: Doctor? Nurse? Lima, Peru? That's a big city! I thought all missionaries lived in jungles in grass huts.

Grandpa: Well, Sammie, some missionaries DO live in jungles. They share God's good news about Jesus with the people who live there. But other missionaries live in towns. Or they even live in large cities like Lima, Peru or London or Paris or New York.

Matthew: But Grandpa, what do missionaries really DO?

Grandpa: *(Chuckles.)* Well, there are as many kinds of jobs as there are missionaries! *(Counts on fingers.)* Missionaries might be doctors or nurses, like my friends. They might be teachers or pastors. They might fly airplanes to bring in supplies or work in book stores that sell books about Jesus. But whatever jobs missionaries do, they do them for the same reason: so that they can tell other people the good news about Jesus!

Sammie: *(Looks down at list.)* Hmmm...I guess I had it all wrong. I'll need to decide what kind of job I can DO, and where I can GO to help people BEFORE I know what things to take with me!

Grandpa: *(Pats SAMMIE on the shoulder.)* Good idea, Sammie. Take it one step at a time. Ask God to show you what you can do to get ready—and do it!

Matthew: Thanks for your help, Grandpa.

Sammie: Yeah, thanks! *(MATTHEW and SAMMIE exit.)*

Grandpa *(waving)***:** Glad to help! Come back anytime. *(Curtain closes.)*

SNACKS

Give your kids a literal taste of what it's like to live in another culture! Far more than just a way to keep kid's faces smiling and tummies full, snacks can be a learning experience. Some of these snack recipes can be used as group learning activities, giving kids a chance to learn to work together as well as the chance to learn cooking skills. Other snack recipes feature ingredients that are native to other parts of the world, giving rise to natural opportunities to talk about the foods and cultures of other countries.

To give a food experience that transcends the simple snack, research the kinds of foods eaten in the country you want to feature. On a trip to the grocery store, see how many ingredients of those foods are available locally. Then prepare one or two of the chosen ethnic dishes ahead of time and also bring the ingredients for a simple recipe that the children can help prepare. A "food night" can be a source of extra understanding—and extra sparkle!

Ants on a Log

Materials Checklist
- celery
- peanut butter
- raisins
- plastic knives
- napkins

How to Use: Wash celery and cut into 2-inch (5-cm) sections—several sections for each child. Spread peanut butter in the center of each section, topping with raisins. **These aren't real ants. But what people groups do eat ants and other insects for protein?** (Australian aborigines, some Africans, etc.) **Why do you think people in our country don't eat insects?** (Chocolate-covered ants are available in some gourmet shops.)

Apple Trees

Materials Checklist
- 1 apple for each child
- stick pretzels
- mild cheddar or jack cheese
- plastic knives
- plastic forks
- napkins

How to Use: Children (or you) wash hands and cut cheese into cubes with plastic knives. Next, children poke pretzels through the skins of their apples (use a plastic fork to make holes if apple skins are tough). Top each pretzel with a cheese chunk.

Banana in a Blanket

Materials Checklist
- 1 banana for each child
- 1 tortilla for each child
- smooth peanut butter
- spoons
- napkins

How to Use: Each child needs a banana, an 8-inch (20-cm) flour tortilla, a spoon, and smooth peanut butter. Child spreads peanut butter on the tortilla, using back of spoon. Child peels banana, lays it on one edge of the tortilla and rolls it up. **In what countries do people eat a lot of tortillas?** (Mexico, South America, United States.) **Do you know where peanuts were first grown?** (Africa.)

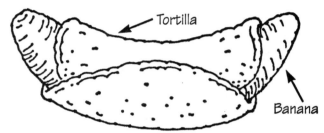

Tortilla

Banana

Banana and Pineapple Kebobs

Materials Checklist
- ½ banana for each child
- pineapple chunks
- toothpicks or bamboo skewers
- plastic knives
- bowl
- napkins

How to Use: Cut bananas into 2-inch sections. Drain canned pineapple chunks. Place fruit in a bowl. Children make kebobs with toothpicks or bamboo skewers. **Where is pineapple grown?** (Hawaii, other tropical countries.)

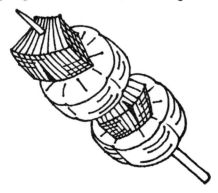

Rice Cakes with Topping

Materials Checklist

◆ rice cakes
◆ peanut butter or cream cheese
◆ knives
◆ napkins

How to Use: Provide one rice cake for each child. Child spreads peanut butter or cream cheese on rice cake. **What countries use rice as their main food?** (China, Japan, India, Mexico, etc.) **What other foods do they eat with rice?**

Honey and Peanut Butter Balls

Materials Checklist

◆ 1 part honey
◆ 1 part peanut butter
◆ 2 parts nonfat dried milk
◆ bowl
◆ wooden spoon

Optional—

◆ crushed cereal

How to Use: Mix honey and peanut butter together until smooth. Add dry milk, a little at a time, to make a dough-like consistency. Form into a large ball. Add a little more honey if mixture is too stiff; add dry milk if too runny.

Children wash hands and pinch off about a teaspoon of dough, rolling dough into a ball. (Optional: Balls may be rolled in crushed cereal flakes before eating.)

Banana Wafers

Materials Checklist

◆ vanilla wafers
◆ 1/3 banana for each child
◆ plastic knives
◆ napkins

How to Use: Using plastic knives, children cut peeled bananas into slices. Put each slice of banana between two vanilla wafers. **What countries grow bananas?** (Most tropical countries.)

Trail Mix

Materials Checklist

◆ nuts (such as walnuts, almonds or peanuts)
◆ sunflower seeds
◆ dates or raisins
◆ small pretzels or cereal pieces
◆ bowl
◆ large spoon
◆ small cups with which to scoop out trail mix

Optional—

◆ chopped unsweetened coconut (from health food stores)
◆ chocolate or carob chips
◆ small marshmallows

How to Use: Children wash hands and put ingredients into a large bowl. Children stir ingredients with large spoon until ingredients are completely mixed, then use small cups to scoop out a portion of snack.

Australian Lamingtons

Materials Checklist

◆ 9x13-inch unfrosted yellow cake,
   cut into 2-inch cubes
◆ 3 cups powdered sugar
◆ 1/3 cup cocoa
◆ 3 tablespoons butter or margarine, melted
◆ 1/2 cup boiling water
◆ 3 cups shredded coconut
◆ measuring utensils
◆ saucepan
◆ bowl
◆ pie tin
◆ spoon
◆ forks
◆ knife
◆ wire rack

Serves 12-15

How to Use: Mix sugar and cocoa in a bowl, then add boiling water and melted butter. Mix well until smooth. Set icing bowl in a saucepan about one-fourth full of simmering water to keep it warm. Place coconut in a pie tin next to the saucepan and a wire rack on the other side of the coconut, in assembly-line fashion. Using forks, dip each square of cake into the hot icing and let the excess icing drip off. Then roll iced cake in coconut on all sides and place on wire rack to cool.

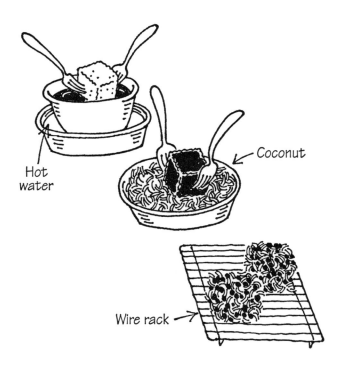

Hot water

Coconut

Wire rack

Burritos

Materials Checklist

◆ 2-4 ounces cheddar cheese
◆ 8-ounce can refried beans
◆ 6 flour tortillas
◆ can opener
◆ large bowl
◆ spoons
◆ grater
◆ microwave oven or electric frying pan

Optional—

◆ black olives
◆ salsa
◆ sour cream
◆ chopped onions
◆ chopped lettuce
◆ chopped mild peppers

Serves 6

How to Use: Children wash hands, grate cheese into bowl and open refried beans (with adult supervision). Adult warms tortillas in microwave or on frying pan. Each child spoons about three tablespoons of refried beans down the center of a tortilla and sprinkles cheese on top, then folds tortilla to cover about one-third of the line of beans and rolling sides of tortilla around filling. An adult heats the burritos in microwave oven (about one minute) or in an electric skillet set to medium. (Optional: Children add other ingredients to burritos.)

What country do burritos come from? (Mexico.) **What other ways do people use tortillas? What other grain are tortillas often made from?** (Corn.)

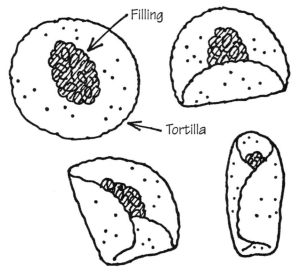

Filling

Tortilla

Chapati

Materials Checklist

◆ 2 cups whole wheat flour
◆ ½ tsp. salt
◆ 2 Tbs. vegetable oil
◆ ½ cup water
◆ rolling pin
◆ waxed paper
◆ measuring utensils
◆ serving plate
◆ mixing bowl and spoon
◆ pastry brush
◆ electric frying pan
◆ spatula

Optional—

◆ butter, cheese spread, jam or honey

Serves 12

How to Use: Children wash hands, then measure flour and salt into a bowl. They measure and add oil, then work it into flour thoroughly with fingers. Children measure and stir in water, then work dough with hands until it holds together. Dough should be kneaded until smooth, about five minutes, in the bowl or on a piece of waxed paper.

Divide dough into 10-12 balls. Children roll balls between waxed paper sheets to make thin circles about 7 inches (17.5 cm) in diameter. *Adult help:* Brush oil onto each chapati and place in electric frying pan set at medium heat. Cook about one minute on each side. If chapati puffs, press down gently with a spatula.

What is one food you think is eaten just about everywhere? Bread of some kind is eaten in most countries of the world every day. Chapati (Chuh-PAH-tee) **is eaten in Africa, the Middle East, India, and many other places!**

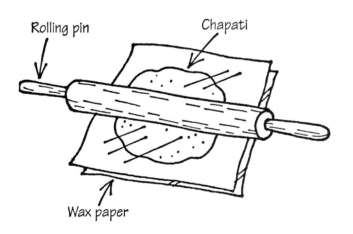

Rolling pin

Chapati

Wax paper

Chow Mein Chewies

Materials Checklist

◆ 12-ounce package butterscotch pieces (like chocolate chips)
◆ ½ cup peanut butter
◆ 6-ounce can of fried chow mein noodles
◆ 1 cup shelled peanuts
◆ measuring cups
◆ large saucepan
◆ wooden spoon
◆ cookie sheet
◆ waxed paper
◆ spoons

Serves 10-12

How to Use: Children place butterscotch pieces and peanut butter in saucepan. Cook on low heat until melted. Remove from heat. Children add noodles and peanuts, then stir well. Line bottom of cookie sheet with waxed paper. Children drop spoonfuls of mixture onto waxed paper. Let stand until firm.

From what country did noodles come from? (China.) **Many people think noodles came from Italy, but Marco Polo brought them from China on his travels. Some noodles are boiled; these noodles were fried to make them crispy.**

Costa Rican Dessert

Materials Checklist

- 2 cups milk
- 1 Tbs. instant decaffeinated coffee
- 2 Tbs. sugar
- ice
- measuring utensils
- 2 blenders or food processors with ice grater capability
- paper cups
- spoons

Optional—

- 2 tsp. vanilla
- 2 tsp. cinnamon

Serves 8

How to Use: With adult supervision, children grate 8 cups of ice and spoon grated ice into cups. Blend milk, decaffeinated coffee, and sugar for 30 seconds or just until blended, but not frothy. (Optional: Add vanilla and cinnamon to liquid.) Pour 1/2 cup of liquid mixture over each cup of ice to make a snow cone. Eat immediately.

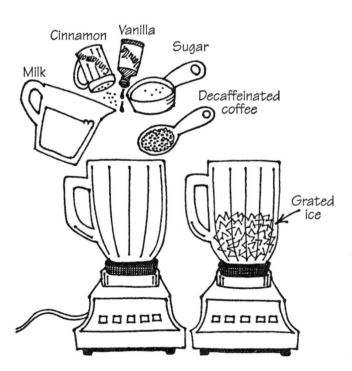

Fresh Fruit with Coconut Dip

Materials Checklist

- fruits such as cantaloupe, papayas, mangoes, tangerines, oranges, apples, strawberries, bananas
- 1/2 cup chopped peanuts
- 1 12-ounce can frozen lemonade, thawed
- 1 cup coconut cream (available at gourmet markets or health food stores)
- spoons
- plastic knives
- measuring cups
- serving plate
- mixing bowl and spoon
- toothpicks
- small paper cups for dip

Serves 12-14

What are some of your favorite desserts? In many countries, people often eat fruit for dessert. Today we're going to make an African dessert from the country of Ghana.

How to Use: Children wash hands, then cut fruit into small chunks and arrange on serving plate, sprinkling with peanuts. Others make the dip by mixing the lemonade and coconut cream, then spooning individual portions into cups. Children spear fruit chunks with toothpicks to dip.

Japanese Bentô Box

Materials Checklist

- 4 cups cooked Japanese rice
- 1/4 cup rice vinegar (or white vinegar)
- 1/2 cup sesame oil (or vegetable oil)
- 1 Tbs. sugar
- toasted sesame seeds
- lettuce
- cucumber
- carrot
- Japanese red pickled ginger (available where Asian foods are sold)
- small shallow box for each child (such as a candy box)
- waxed paper
- grater
- measuring cups
- aluminum foil
- green construction paper
- scissors
- 2 mixing bowls
- mixing spoon
- vegetable cutting knives
- a set of chopsticks for each child

Serves 6

How to Use: Children wash hands and grate carrot, slice cucumber and shred lettuce, then combine vegetables with pickled ginger in a bowl. Children mix vinegar, oil and sugar together in a second bowl, pour it over vegetables and ginger, tossing gently to cover. On a sheet of wax paper, each child shapes 1/2 cup of rice into a triangle. (If rice is dry, shape with wet hands.) Child sprinkles sesame seeds on the outside edge of the rice triangle.

Each child lines the inside of the bottom of his or her box with foil, pinching to make a wall in the center of the bottom, then pinching foil tightly around the edge of the box. Child places rice triangle in one part of lunch box and adds some of the vegetable mixture in the other part. Child cuts construction paper "sprigs of grass" and places them in the box with the rice triangle. Take bentô boxes and chopsticks outside for a Japanese-style picnic.

Japanese workers often buy box lunches called cal bentô (kahl BEHN toh). A bentô box is divided into sections. Each section holds a different food that is attractively arranged.

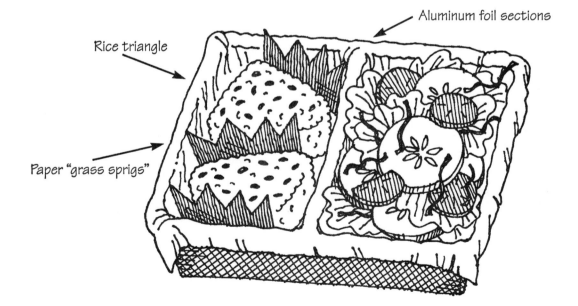

Rice triangle

Aluminum foil sections

Paper "grass sprigs"

Japanese Pineapple Cream Dessert

Materials Checklist

◆ 2 envelopes unflavored gelatin
◆ 2 cups water
◆ 2 cups milk
◆ 3/4 cup sugar
◆ 1 teaspoon almond extract
◆ 1 fresh pineapple, cut into cubes
◆ measuring utensils
◆ saucepan
◆ wooden spoon
◆ 9-inch square cake pan
◆ knife

Serves 8-10

How to Use: In a saucepan, sprinkle gelatin over 1/2 cup cold water; stir until dissolved. Add remaining water, the milk and sugar. Heat, stirring frequently, until mixture begins to set, then add almond extract, stirring well. Pour mixture into a 9-inch square cake pan and chill in the freezer to set quickly. Cut dessert into 1-inch cubes and serve along with cubes of pineapple. (If making recipe with children, do cooking step early in the program to allow time for dessert to set.)

Russian Two-Cheese Salad

Materials Checklist

◆ 1 12-ounce brick white cheese (such as Jack or Gouda)
◆ 1 12-ounce brick yellow cheese (such as mild cheddar)
◆ garlic salt
◆ green onions
◆ 2 boiled eggs
◆ 1/2 cup sour cream
◆ 1 loaf brown bread (Russian rye or pumpernickel)
◆ several knives
◆ bowl
◆ wooden spoon
◆ napkins or paper plates
◆ cheese graters
◆ cutting boards

Serves 8-10

How to Use: Children grate the cheeses, chop onions and eggs. Mix cheeses, onions, eggs and sour cream. Each child spreads cheese salad on a slice of bread and may sprinkle garlic salt on top of mixture. (Encourage children to sprinkle garlic salt on just a corner and taste it to see if they like it before sprinkling it on the whole mixture.)

CLIP ART

Clip art can be a wonderful way to enhance and decorate fliers, church bulletins, folders, forms and posters. But clip art can do more than just decorate—it can help to clearly put across the message of your words! That appropriate picture is truly worth a thousand words!

Also included are some "instant poster" forms (pp. 125-133). Just enlarge and color them as you wish, add the necessary information and post—all in just a few minutes' time!

Helping Hands

Hey, Kids!

THE GREAT KIDMISSION • 127

Where:

When:

The Great KidMission

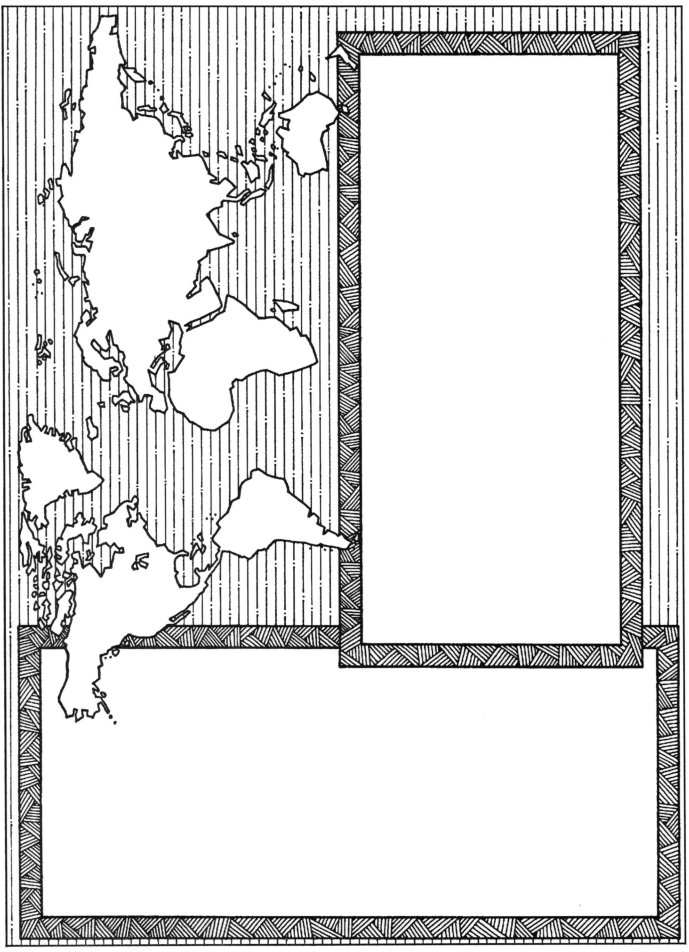

The Great KidMission Conference

The Great KidMission Conference

The Great KidMission Conference

Good News

Good News

Good News

HELP WANTED

HELP WANTED

HELP WANTED

Kids are Special People!

Kids in Action

Kids are Special People!

KIDS IN ACTION

Kids in Action

KIDS ARE SPECIAL PEOPLE!

LISTEN UP

LISTEN UP

Listen Up

MISSIONS MONTH

Missions Month

Kids' Missions Conference

Kids' Missions Conference

MISSIONS MONTH

MISSIONS WEEK

MISSIONS WEEK

Missions Week

MARK YOUR CALENDAR

MARK YOUR CALENDAR

Mark Your Calendar

APPENDIX

Here is a brief appendix to help you
find out more about some people
groups and countries around
the world where your
missionaries might be serving.

INFORMATION, PLEASE!

The people groups and countries listed below are served by many Christian mission agencies. Some of these agencies are listed below by their acronyms. These acronyms are keyed to the agency names and addresses found on p. 139. Write to these agencies for information about mission work being done among the following people groups or in the countries below:

PEOPLE GROUP	AGENCY	COUNTRY	AGENCY
Azeri	WEC YWAM	Albania	PI YWAM
Baluch	IVS WBT WEC	Bhutan	LM YWAM
Children	PI TEAM	Chad	MAF TEAM WBT WEC
Dogon	WBT	Djibouti	RSMT
Euskaldunak	EURO	Ethiopia	PI
Falasha	SIM	Fiji	WEC YWAM
Gypsies	EURO	Greece	BCU
Herero	AIM MAF	Haiti	WGM OMS
Jola	WEC	Indonesia	PI TEAM
Kurds	WBT WEC	Japan	PI WGM
Lobi	WBT WEC	Korea (South)	OMS KACWM TEAM
Minangkabau	IMF OMF	Lesotho	AIM
Navajo	WBT NGM	Mongolia	MAF TEAM WEC
Parsees	IS	New Zealand	YWAM
Quecha	PI WBT	Oman	AWM
San (Bushmen)	MAF YWAM	Papua New Guinea	WBT YWAM
Tibetans	WEC TEAM	Romania	PI TEAM
Uzbek	WEC	Sri Lanka	PI TEAM WEC
Vagla	WBT WEC	Turkey	PI TEAM
Wolof	SIM WBT WEC	United Arab Emirates	TEAM WEC
Yao	PI OMF	Venezuela	TEAM
Zulu	PI TEAM	Xinjiang-China	PI WEC
		Zimbabwe	PI TEAM

Taken from YOU CAN CHANGE THE WORLD by Jill Johnstone.
Copyright © 1992 by Jill Johnstone. Used by permission of Zondervan Publishing House.

CHRISTIAN AGENCIES
Address List

Contact these missions agencies for information about their ministries
and the people groups or countries they serve as listed on p. 138.

AIM
Africa Inland Mission International, Inc.
P. O. Box 178
Pearl River, NY   10965

AWM
Arab World Ministries
P.O. Box 96
Upper Darby, PA   19082

BCU
Bible Christian Union, Inc.
P.O. Box 410
Hatfield, PA   19440-0410

EURO
Euromission
Postbus 32
3950 AC Maarn,
The Netherlands

FRO
Frontiers
Jill Harris
Coordinator of Children's Missions Education
325 North Stapley Dr.
Mesa, AZ   85203

IMF
Indonesian Missionary Fellowship
P.O. Box 4, Batu 65301
E. Java, Indonesia

IS
Interserve
239 Fairfield Ave.
P.O. Box 418
Upper Darby, PA   19082

IVS
Mr. Irving Sylvia
18134 Woodbarn Lane
Fountain Valley, CA   92708

KACWM
Korean American Society for World Mission
1605 Elizabeth St.
Pasadena, CA   91104

LM
Leprosy Mission International
Goldhay Way,
Orton Goldhay,
Peterborough,
PE2 OGZ, England

MAF
Mission Aviation Fellowship
P.O. Box 3202
Redlands, CA   92373

NGM
Navajo Gospel Mission
P.O. Box 3717
Flagstaff, AZ   86003

OMF
Overseas Missionary Fellowship
404 S. Church St.
Robesonia, PA   19551

OMS
OMS International
P.O. Box A
Greenwood, IN   46142

PI
Partners International
P. O. Box 15025
San Jose, CA   95115-0025

RSMT
Red Sea Mission Team
P. O. Box 16227
Minneapolis, MN   55416

SIM
Society for International Ministries
P. O. Box 7900
Charlotte, NC   28241

TEAM
The Evangelical Alliance Mission
P. O. Box 969
Wheaton, IL   60189-0969

WBT
Wycliffe Bible Translators International
7500 West Camp Wisdom Road
Dallas, TX   75326

WEC
WEC International
P.O. Box 1707
Fort Washington, PA   19034-8707

WGM
World Gospel Mission
P.O. Box WGM
Marion, IN   46952

YWAM
Youth With a Mission
P.O. Box 55309
Seattle, WA   98155

INDEXES

The indexes are here to help you find what you're looking for as well as to help you combine Bible stories, snacks and activities to customize each day's program. Besides being indexed alphabetically, activities are indexed by country. A Scripture index is also included to help coordinate each day's Bible story with the lesson themes.

ALPHABETICAL INDEX

ACTIVITIES
Indexed by Continent

SCRIPTURE INDEX
for Bible Stories